PRESSUREPOINT
ADVERSITIES STRENGTHEN AND PUSH YOU TO YOUR DESTINY

Maria,

Thank you so much
for the support. I
pray my words encourage
you to live through
purpose.

Love,

About the Author

There is always more than a title that makes a person. Meet Jenny Thelwell. She has many roles to accomplish every day - Life coach. Doctoral student. Educator. Mother. Wife. Daughter. Sister. Friend. Soldier. Survivor. Child of God. Her first book, Pressure Point, is Jenny's transparent memoir about how she learned to convert trauma into victory. A survivor of sexual abuse, Jenny lives to teach others how to progress from victim of any circumstance to victor.

Jenny's life experiences built the foundation for Revolutionary Diamond, and Revolutionary Diamond gave Jenny the platform to be a life coach and change lives with her story. With a passion for expression, Jenny not only published her first book, Pressure Point, but she took it a step further and became a Writing coach, to help women like herself write their masterpieces with confidence.

Your story is more important than you know, and sometimes it just takes the right person to listen and an even more courageous person to tell it. The time is NOW!

We all have a story to tell. What's yours?

"EMBRACE THE PRESSURE!"

Cover Photography from Leon Lloyd, Stop Playin Studio

Edited by The Comprehensive Editing, Writing & Publishing Company, LLC, Raleigh, NC

Formatted by John Edgar Design @ http://JohnEdgar.Design

Acknowledgements

There is no such thing as 'making it' alone. No one knows this better than I. I am here because many people were in my corner listening to me, laughing with me, crying with me, holding me, cheering for me, praying for me, lifting me up, and holding me accountable.

To my daughter, please forgive me for the countless minutes I missed spending time with my family as I focused on achieving my life goals. However, I hope that I have inspired you, that I have ignited in you a fire that man will never blow out. My success will be measured solely by yours.

To my husband, you held me down through most of my endeavors. I am forever grateful for your patience and for the hard work you did day in and day out for our family.

To my beloved CS, y'all already know how I feel about y'all. You only see me in your DMs and in iMessage almost 100 times a day, every day. Your motivation and understanding of me, a crazy, sometimes lost, sometimes found human being is unmatched. I value our sistership more than you will ever know.

To my church family, you have made Sundays my favorite day of the week! Thank you for the guidance and the spirit that embodies that temple every time I walk in it. I'm giving birth to a new thing. God's doing a new thing. I'm ready for the overflow.

To Mom and my family, some things in this book you guys had no idea about, and that's okay. This is my journey, my truth, my story. God intended my life to happen as it has. This is part of His will for my life, and because of that, I've made my life and myself open and available in hopes of helping another. Philippian's 2:13 says, "for it is God who works in you to will and to act in order to fulfill his good purpose" (NIV).

To those reading this book, I pray you find comfort. I pray you find purpose. I pray you find courage. Most of all, I pray you have found God. Because I may fail you, but He never will.

PRESSUREPOINT

ADVERSITIES STRENGTHEN AND PUSH YOU TO YOUR DESTINY

by
Jenny Thelwell

Contents

Introduction

I grew up with a loving yet toxic father. Weird how those two adjectives can go together. When Papi wasn't drinking, he was so much fun to be around. We could play for hours, and I enjoyed every second of being with him. He had a way of making me feel like I was the only one that mattered. I was the apple of his eye. But as I grew older, Papi drank more often. Playtime was replaced with more and more heated, loud arguments between him and my mother. Their profanity-laced 'discussions' became the norm for our home. As a kid, I wondered, 'Is this how my life is going to be from now on? Is this all there is to life? Will I ever get past these times?'

For what seemed an eternity, I felt completely stuck. Then, things changed for me. I'll tell you how in the pages to come, but for now, I want to ask you a few soul-searching questions. Do you feel like there has to be more to life than what you're getting out of it right now? Do you think as I did growing up—stuck? Or, even though others in your circle have found success, you believe you have been through so much

d

you will never see success. Are you in search of your purpose? If your answers to any of these questions are "yes," then I am here to tell you that you are awesome. You are special. You are hand-picked to do that very thing you keep doubting that you can do!

At times, you may feel like the odds are stacked against you, and that my dear friend, maybe true. However, before God put you in this world, He impregnated you with a vision, a purpose, or that dream you keep dreaming. Whatever you want to call it, your purpose comes with signs that keep finding you. For example, maybe it's a business that you keep talking about. If that's the case, then that is your baby. Yes, you are pregnant with possibilities! It is your job to nourish that baby, to learn as much as you can about it, to birth that baby, and then develop it. Without a doubt, it will be hard, it will be grueling, but it will be worth the sleepless nights, putting up with the constant naysayers, and enduring the financial hardships to keep it going. If you hold on, if you keep going, if you plan and work at fulfilling your vision, you will prevail. God will fulfill all the desires of your heart because when you birth that baby, you will touch many and bring glory to our Lord. Don't fret. Instead, know that He is God and that the journey to birth that baby will reveal many things to you. In your journey is where your purpose lies, which is that baby! Enjoy the journey. Ride the waves!

Regardless of the many crooked roads and the many stop signs, you will see on your way, remember, there would be no testimony without a test. We are all tested. As one writer put it, everything we do is a test. However, no test lasts forever. So, exhale. All shall be well. I should know. I am a Latina woman who grew up in America, a place where opportunities abound. As I intimated before, my life was not an easy one. But I found my way to success, and in this book, I explain how it happened for me and how things can change for you, too. Read on to find out.

Chapter 1
In the Beginning...

As a Latina in America, I often wonder how I got this far. I was born and raised in a poor neighborhood in South Miami, to an alcoholic father and a wonderful, hard-working, supportive mother. Because my father used his paycheck to fund his drinking more than he did our household, our home was one that struggled to make ends meet. Even after he and my mother would argue tirelessly and she decided she and us kids should leave the house, things didn't get any better any time soon. Mami did the best she could, but there were many, many days we had to do without. In a word, times were not 'easy' for us.

Today, I sit in an office with a secretary and teachers following my lead. Yet, I still feel like that little girl. The girl who rode the bus to Dunbar Elementary School. The girl who couldn't ride in the comfort of a car, like other classmates. I walked to the neighborhood corner store amid smelly, stumbling alcoholics while stepping over drug addicts before I even got to the store to purchase some candy. And this was an everyday routine first thing in the morning before the bell rang for school to

d

start.

As I said before, for many years, success eluded me. There were seasons in my life where I felt I was lost. I was going through the motions, just trying to do what I thought was right by upholding the values and morals my mother instilled in me. The older I got, the more apparent it was that every struggle has a purpose and that those struggles propelled me to where I am today, even to the point of writing this book. I am a living witness that no matter where you are in life, God will meet you there and plant pebbles along the way. I didn't know it then, and just like you, I didn't understand it. But I didn't give up and you can't either.

MY LIFE IN SO MANY WORDS

If I can do it—a poor Latina raised by immigrant parents in the tough streets of Miami; literally, anyone can! I wrote this book to inspire others who, like me, have the odds stacked against them and feel like they may not be able to make it. I am a living witness that if you do move forward by faith and continue to work on your dreams, you can make those dreams a reality.

Currently, as a doctoral candidate, it was important for me to understand my educational journey and where this anticipated degree will take me professionally. One place that working on this degree has taken me is into the world of publishing this book. For me, Pressure Point is my story and my way of inspiring others. This book is a totally different project and life-changing experience, not just for me but for others. When I share with family and friends that I am working on my dissertation and writing a book at the same time, their favorite line is,

"You have got to be crazy to write a book and a dissertation at the same time." To which I answer, "Yes, I am. How dare I use my time wisely and dedicate all of it to serve others through literature?"

To encourage myself in my journey to an advanced degree, I researched what it means to be a "doctoral" candidate. According to the dictionary, it means "designed to achieve." That spoke to me. I am designed to achieve, not because the dictionary said so. But because God said so. The dictionary's definition only confirmed it.

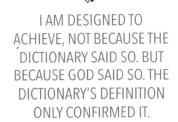

I AM DESIGNED TO ACHIEVE, NOT BECAUSE THE DICTIONARY SAID SO. BUT BECAUSE GOD SAID SO. THE DICTIONARY'S DEFINITION ONLY CONFIRMED IT.

SO, WHAT'S THE PROBLEM?

From my doctoral studies, I learned that a dissertation has a problem statement that describes the reason why a study needs to be done to solve a problem or preferably find a solution to a common practice. My problem was that I was a minority growing up in America. Consequently, I had encounters specific to growing up in a country that does not always welcome ethnic groups. At the same time, my problem, if you will, is an inspirational one because it fostered within me a drive to continue to tread pathways that seemingly were never meant for minorities to walk. The thing is there is a process that one must endure first. And, there is no way around it. My case was no different, and neither will yours.

Consider the butterfly. Now, every butterfly was once a caterpillar, right? The journey to blossoming into a beautiful creature is amazing. Still, the process is many times underestimated, if not underappreciated altogether. There are stages in which the caterpillar undergoes that must be accomplished to become the beautiful creature we see. Before its transformation, however, no one really cares to see a caterpillar. Slick and large, it is a yucky, small crawling creature that does absolutely nothing but scoot in whatever direction it's headed. Oh, but when a caterpillar becomes a butterfly, everyone o-o-h's and a-a-h's at it. It has beautiful bright, colorful wings. It flies all over with a kind of flutter. It is even said that if one gets close to you, it will bring you good luck! Not too many positive things are said about the caterpillar. When you hear someone say, "It feels like I have butterflies in my stomach," do you envision caterpillars crawling inside that person's stomach? Or do you picture butterflies fluttering inside?

Herein lies a problem in our society. Sticking with the analogy of the butterfly, let's say that people love to see the butterfly flutter about in its beauty. Yet, they fail to see the hard work it took the caterpillar to transform itself into a beautiful creature. People forget that beauty went through a necessary process that did not happen overnight. Similarly, some people tend to surmise your success born out of pure luck. They may even think you were spoon-fed success by your parents or that someone must have "hooked" you up. They don't see all the sweat and tears you spent sowing, working, studying during the late nights and the early mornings. They only see the glory and only want to be around during harvest season. That is, they do not want to plant and believe in your dream before it comes to fruition.

Every stage of the caterpillar requires a different mindset, a repositioning. There are so many things we can learn in every stage of our lives. Here is another problem that hinders us from appreciating every stage of growth. As humans, we tend to want to get to the finish line fast. We tend to take shortcuts to fast forward to the end. But there is a lesson in every step to the finish line. Shortcuts will have you miss the steps every time. Admittedly, most times, we do not know where or what the finish line looks like. So how do we know what to look for? It's just a feeling, right? The feeling of finally "making it," but what does "making it" feel like if we do not complete all the steps to the finish line?

At various points in my life, I felt that feeling—that feeling of "making it." However, that feeling was short-lived. Many accomplishments in life, like winning a track meet, graduating from high school, and college, giving birth to my daughter, and getting married—gave me the feeling of having "made it." But did I really? The answer is no. It was tough getting that degree, but the real work comes afterward when I succeeded in getting a job but realized I was still broke! Eventually, I had to learn that what you do with those steppingstones is what will ultimately show you what your purpose is.

IN THE BEGINNING, THERE IS PURPOSE.

From the millisecond, you were a thought in the mind of God. There has been a purpose attached to you. Do you have any idea what it is? How do you know what your purpose is? How do you keep going after you feel like you've just given all you have? This is the problem. We do not always know how to tap into what our gifts and/or talents are. Therefore, we get lost and feel sorry for ourselves. I learned very soon that finishing the first degree was just a short-term goal that would propel me to my next stage and the next one after that until I would ultimately achieve my purpose. In other words, getting my degree was not the end goal. It was a necessary stage to proceed. As great as it felt to get the degree, it was not the icing on the cake or the cake for that matter. It was just part of the foundation of what was to come. So again, what is your purpose? Why are you doing what you're doing right now? Why are you at that job? What do you think about your future? Your answers may just help you decipher what God Himself had in mind from the beginning when He created you.

It wasn't until my senior year in college that I started asking myself those same questions. At the time, I was just trying to finish up in any major. That's exactly what I did. Imagine how lost I was. I was going with the flow. I finally graduated with a degree in Mass Media Communications. I was going to be a reporter! A news anchor no less!

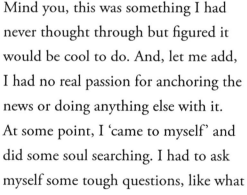

EVERYTHING YOU HAVE ENCOUNTERED IN YOUR LIFE HAS PURPOSE AND IS A PART OF GOD'S PLAN FOR THE UNIMAGINABLE LIFE HE HAS FOR YOU.

Mind you, this was something I had never thought through but figured it would be cool to do. And, let me add, I had no real passion for anchoring the news or doing anything else with it. At some point, I 'came to myself' and did some soul searching. I had to ask myself some tough questions, like what did I have passion for? I began searching for that answer for a while, and I am glad to report (no pun intended) that I have found it!

As you continue reading, I want you to keep something in mind. Everything you have encountered in your life has purpose and meaning and is a part of God's plan to prepare you for the unimaginable life He has for you.

The stories in the next chapters are true. As painful as it was for me to recount them to you, I have relived these moments for only one purpose. I want to let you know that regardless of present circumstances, salvation in every sense of that word is the only way to find your purpose. You will get 'unstuck.' Meanwhile, make peace with your past (and present) and find the good in each situation. Let the Word of God assure you that everything you've encountered, every acquaintance you've met, every wicked or nice boss you've had is working together for your good right now (Romans 8:28).

Chapter 1
Questions

How did you perceive your life while going through daily struggles when you were younger? Were you able to see a brighter future at the time? If so, how?

At this very moment in your life, are you where you pictured you would be? If yes, how did you get there? If not, what can you do now to get there?

As you reflect on your life, do you feel God was there in the midst of your struggles? In a few sentences, reflect on how you know He was there or why you think He wasn't.

In retrospect, what have you learned about the beginning stages of your life?

Overall, Chapter One Reflections

Chapter 2
Count It All Joy

*"Count it all joy, my brothers, when you
meet trials of various kinds"*
- James 1:2, ESV

DADDY'S GIRL

Papi was a fair-skinned man with soft, black wavy hair and green eyes. He was so tall that he towered over most of our family and friends. I often joked that he wasn't a real Dominican because his fair skin wasn't anything like the dark hue that Dominicans have, including most members of our family. As a little girl, I loved everything about this tall, handsome giant. In my young wisdom, he could do no wrong. And, if I ever did see an issue—like the way he spoke abrasively to Mami—I would come up with hundreds of reasons to excuse his behaviors. Anyone with the nerve to disagree with me about Papi's virtues immediately became my enemy. Papi was always right, and no one could convince me differently, not even Mami. He was my first love, my protector, my shield, my knight in shining armor. My father was so important to me at an early age that I defined my self-worth by his opinions. I would flaunt every new dress, every new hairstyle in front of him, and wait anxiously for his approval. I needed him and wanted him

d

to be in my life forever. We had a special bond, one which I swore as a little girl would never end.

Too bad I couldn't close my eyes and click my heels twice to see into the future.

EXIT THE MAKE-BELIEVE WORLD, ENTER THE REAL ONE

As an adolescent, I knew everything that was going on even though the adults tried to hide it from me. For example, one year, my father was gone for an extended period of time. My mom told me he was working away on a ship. Somehow, I learned that wasn't true. He was actually incarcerated in the Bahamas from a drug bust that occurred on the ship he worked on at the time. I never really got all the details, but what else was there to really know? He was gone and I knew where he was. What I thought was a happy home was changing. With Papi gone, things that should've been his responsibilities (like helping Mami raise my younger siblings) shifted to me. And, things that parents should share between each other (like bringing in income for the home) rested solely on Mami. As a cosmetologist, she earned a living for us with long hours and hard work. I was proud of her hustle and am still amazed at how strong and how alive her spirit was back then and still is to this day.

Life (as I knew it) in our house grew steadily unstable, especially between my parents. They had this huge argument that I told you about earlier, which became the beginning of the ending of their marriage. It also ushered in the undoing of the bond between Papi and me, except I didn't know it then. Anyway, after they separated, Mami had a hard time meeting the bills and making sure us kids had something to eat.

It got so bad that even a simple meal of pork-and-beans and hot dogs would do just fine back then, but now many nights meal was a bowl of cereal.

When my dad and my mom separated, my mom checked in to a live-in rehabilitation center for drug addiction, and my brother and I moved in with our father since he had been released from jail. Things were okay for the most part; that is, at least no hollering and accusations were going back and forth between Mami and Papi. However, we worried about our mom. Sometime later, my brother was able to live with her at the rehabilitation center. She took him with her, leaving me with Papi. I wished I could have gone to live with her as well, but I was glad my brother went. Papi had given him the choice of staying or going with Mami. He chose Mami. It was my dad's way of treating him like a man. That is, he allowed my five-year-old brother to make a significant life-changing decision on his own, to decide where he would live. Trouble was my brother was not an adult. He was just a little kid who needed a dad to treat him like one, not like a grown man. But that was the type of man my father was. He ran a tight ship, although he wasn't all that put together himself. He did have a humorous side though and he was caring in his own way, but my brother never really got to see much of that. He only lived in the home with us a few months and then he was gone. They never really developed a father-son relationship. And I am pretty sure that has affected my brother in a significant way. I felt my brother should've stayed with my dad to develop male qualities, and I could've gone with my mother, being a female, but it wasn't my choice.

Once my mother completed a year of her drug rehab program, she moved in with my grandmother and took us with her. She was working, we were together again, and life seemed good. The only one missing from the bunch was Papi. He had tried to get back together with my mom, even though he was living with his girlfriend (tuh!). Mami said she was "done with him." We remained at my grandmother's house long enough for Mami to save to buy a house. I remember being so proud of her. She fought hard to be a provider, a survivor, a mother. In a way, her greatest strength was a woman with discernment, a woman who knew when enough was enough and then having the courage to take the steps needed to move forward and turn her life around for the better.

During their time of separation, Papi came around less and less. Financially, he became no help at all. We were in dire straits for money. She could not shake the feeling that he was holding on to some funds. So, Mami decided to do something very dangerous. Since I still had a key to his house, she set a day and time when we would make our way over there and search for money. Once we were inside, we quickly looked for his checkbook. We found it under his mattress, along with some folders that held important-looking documents. Wasting no time, we scooped everything up and hurried out and headed back to my grandmother's. As soon as we reached safety, Mami took a more careful look inside the folders. In one of them, she found the shock of her life! They were papers finalizing a divorce between her and Papi. "Altagracia De Jesus-DelosSantos y Fausto DelosSantos fueron divorciados en Santo Domingo, Republica Dominicana." My father had gone to the Dominican Republic and divorced her there. To this day, I'm not sure how that was possible since they were married in the United States. Nevertheless, the divorce is legal and recognized here in the states. Savage!!! She was divorced and didn't even know it! The craziest thing about this is that my grandfather divorced my grandmother the same way! Talk about generational curses (we'll talk a little more about this later).

SEEING PAPI IN A DIFFERENT LIGHT

Some years later, my father moved to New York with his girlfriend. It was bad enough, hardly ever seeing him when he lived in the same town and only minutes away. Now he was states apart. The distance significantly reduced any serious contact we'd have with each other. If it hadn't been for the monthly phone calls that I made to him, we would never have talked again. Imagine not having your own father around to celebrate life with you as you achieved one milestone after the other. For me, I felt cheated of his presence. He didn't even show up for my high school graduation—even after I reminded him about it during the monthly phone calls.

Admittedly, he and I really didn't have much to talk about. In all honesty, the conversations were forced and awkward. I remember being furious with him for always being a no-show at my accomplishments. Yet I would not let myself dwell on the disappointments too much be-cause I had bigger fish to fry like passing my college classes, paying rent, and performing as an athlete so I could keep my scholarship. He had no idea about the amount of work I was putting in and probably didn't care. Nevertheless, I wanted to make him proud of me. Even if I had no clue what I wanted to be when I grew up or how I would get there nor had anyone to guide me through college, I had to graduate and make something of myself.

During my senior year of college, I got a surprising call from my aunt in New York. My father had been living with her for some time. Apparently, his girlfriend had left him and moved back to the Dominican Republic to be with her husband. It's funny how life works out. Papi divorced my mother without her knowledge, lived with his girlfriend for over 10 years. Only to find out she had a husband the whole time. Served him right. Anyway, my aunt explained that my father, whom we hadn't seen for seven years, was sick and that we must do our best to come to see him as soon as possible. The news of his being sick made me uneasy, so I made arrangements for my brother and me to fly to New York as quickly as possible.

When my brother and I walked into our aunt's apartment, my father saw us and almost fell. I think he was shocked to see his children and was in disbelief that we were there. After all, we had not seen him in years. As I write this, I think now Papi was embarrassed because he knew he should have made an effort to come to see his children.

He looked different. He was no longer the tall, handsome man with piercing eyes I remembered from my past. He looked weak. I learned that he had a stroke, which permanently affected his brain. He was diagnosed with some form of brain atrophy, which impaired his balance and, at times, his speech. I could not hold back the tears. Remembering who he was when I was a little girl and looking at what he had become made me cry. The visit with this once handsome, strong man who used to hoist me onto his shoulders became quite traumatic for me.

On the other hand, my brother sat emotionless. He even asked why I was crying. He had no emotion or feelings for this man. I couldn't blame him. Even my father commented that he would not have recognized his own son without someone else pointing him out to him. "What a disgrace," I thought to myself. I prayed that the two days I was there to go by fast, and they did. We flew back to Miami, and after that visit, I tried to keep in contact as much as possible.

CARING FOR PAPI, THE STRANGER

Graduation day from college finally arrived. I flew my dad to Miami to celebrate with me. I anticipated being recognized for everything I had been working hard for the past four years. I walked across the stage in my graduation gown! I was so proud that day, and I wasn't the only one. According to my mom, my dad was a mess in the stands crying his eyes out. My mother had to order my brother to watch over him and make sure he was okay throughout the ceremony. I felt so grateful. Through it all, I had my entire family under one roof, and I gave God all the glory.

A few days later, my dad flew back to New York, and I continued to stay in contact with him. As usual, our conversations were strained, but I continued to touch base to ensure he was doing okay. Because I was the child and he was the parent, Papi made up the rule that I should be the one to call. "You're supposed to call me," he said. His expectation was that I should do so practically every other day. If I didn't, he became annoyed with me. And that's exactly what calling him became, responsibility rather than an act from genuine affection. I detested having to call because our conversations were robotic. And I hated when I missed calling three or four days because that meant Papi would have an attitude, followed up with questions about my not calling. Sometimes I would get bold and ask him why he didn't call me instead. I would try to speak about different things during one of my 'robo' calls to him, but he was very dry. He would have the same joke, and we would laugh for a couple of seconds. The more we spoke, the less we laughed. Often, I found myself smirking from a sarcastic response I made in my head to one or two comments he would make. It was all I could do to keep from repeating what I was really thinking.

From one of our brief conversations, I learned he and my aunt were not getting along. I wasn't interested in getting in the middle of it. So when she called me this particular day, I let it go to voicemail. Basically, she blamed me for not caring for him and let loose a long list of derogatory names she had given me. Her message went on to say she had grown tired of him and that she was kicking him out. She complained that he smelled and didn't like to take showers. From that, the list went on and on.

That night, Papi called and told me that he was about to sleep somewhere in the streets of New York because he could no longer stay there. As he was speaking, I heard my aunt in the background, yelling and cussing. At one point, she must've gotten close to him because he screamed, thinking she was going to hit him. I told him to catch a cab to the airport and that I was going to purchase a flight for him.

Have you ever had one of those moments where you made a significant decision without thinking through all of the moving pieces? Well, that is what I did. I sent for my father without considering all the other major stuff going on in my own life. At that point, I had a family of my own to take care of. I was a struggling teacher, and my husband and I had just moved our family to Greensboro, North Carolina. Since it was summertime, we had traveled back home to visit family in Miami, where we stayed at my mom's. On top of all that, here I was buying my father, my mom's ex-husband, a flight to stay there as well while I ironed out his living situation.

I did not have the funds to buy him a plane ticket out of my own money; therefore, I used my daughter's account, which my husband and I started when she was born. Can you imagine borrowing money from a 4-year old? Ludicrous, right? Yikes!

Anyhow, I managed to get him down to Miami and stay at my mom's place while my sister and I scoured Queens to find him an affordable room to rent. Once she and I settled on a place, we bought a bed and all the essentials. He didn't have much, but at least he would not be on the streets. He had a bed, sheets, towels, a phone, and I even set up a weekly meal plan for him at a restaurant that was in the corner of the street where he was to live. It was no easy task to get him situated, but it had to be done. I could not help but think that I was doing more for him in one week than he had done for me in the last twelve years. However, I wanted to ensure that I left him in the best possible position I could, considering he could barely walk on his own.

The place we found for my dad was a temporary fix, with the understanding that he would apply for Section 8. This would give him access to a better dwelling, which was more accommodating to his health condition. However, Papi went on to live in that same place for about four years! While he lived there, his health deteriorated, despite the home health aide he received and other government assistance that was available to him. The windowless room he occupied was in a basement. He shared the bathroom and the kitchen with three other people. This was considered typical New York living for a single person, but it was not a good fit for him. Going up and down the stairs was very hard for him. Even the landlord became very worried about him possibly falling down the steps and wanted him to find somewhere that was better suited for his condition.

At the time, my husband and I were blessed to purchase a four-bedroom home in North Carolina. After talking it over several times, we agreed to offer my father a room in our new home. I knew this would change the dynamic of our family, but I wanted to help because I knew it was the right thing to do. "Honor your father and your mother, that your days may belong in the land that the Lord your God is giving you" (Exodus 20:12). This is one of our Lord's commandments. I knew it would be weird and awkward and that I would have to make some adjustments to how we lived as a family, but it was something I had to do. I had grown to be a very spiritual person, and the church was at the forefront of my life. Subsequently, I felt that asking him to move in with us was my duty as his daughter and as a child of God. Not because he was an awesome father and we had a great relationship, but because God tells us in the great book that we should honor our parents. For at least a year, he resisted our offer until he could turn us down no more. His declining health necessitated better care so he could no longer act on pride and agreed to the move.

I had to learn so much about his health condition and his disability benefits. One of the things I learned is that there is a significant gap between the assistance New York gives the disabled and what North Carolina grants. New York provides so much more. In North Carolina, he barely qualified for the minimal services he did receive. Most importantly, he didn't qualify to have a home health aide, so I had to do almost everything for him. I thank God to this day, however, that I was spared from having to take him a bath. I'm sure I would've gotten through that too, but I rather not have had to do it.

It seemed as though Papi had countless health issues. I had to find a physician, a urologist, a cardiologist, and a neurologist for him to see on a periodical basis. I also had to call and coordinate his doctor appointments and take him because the transportation service never had anyone who spoke Spanish, and that was an ordeal on its own. I had to take him grocery shopping with me as well. Though it doesn't seem like much of a big deal, getting a walker in the trunk and then getting him in the car to then park in front of the store, turn on the intermittent lights, go in the store to hopefully find an electrical cart, to then ride it outside so he can sit in it was a TASK! Sometimes, we would have to wait in the car until an electrical cart was unoccupied. One time, we got tired of waiting, and we decided that he would go into the store using his walker, and let's just say, we never did that again!

When I tried to make light of all that was going on, Papi's negative demeanor and attitude made it all the more difficult for me. He was bitter and complained about his condition all the time. No matter what I did or what struggles he saw me go through to get him situated, it seemed like it was not good enough. Even when he said, "thank you," it seemed forced and unappreciative. I thought to myself, well, it's tough not being able to do what you once used to do. Maybe he just needs some time, perhaps he's depressed. I mean, who wouldn't be. You used to be the man, and now you're all alone. Here I was making excuses for the man who left me, his little girl, when I needed him the most. Not only did I make excuses for him, but also there I was taking care of his every need without him even asking. I anticipated his every want and need and made it happen sacrificing the comfort and time of my own family. While I relived my feelings about him from when I was a little girl, I was fully aware of who this man was with all his faults and shortcomings. Yet, I thought, I am here for you. Isn't this the same thing I did for men I dated...making excuses for why they said or did the things they did to me?

As women, we do not realize that our fathers either hurt us or help us. That is, we subconsciously treat men in our lives the way we treated our father or the way we would have treated him had he been in our life from the beginning. We seem to hold on to the vision we have created in our heads about what a man is supposed to do or how they are to treat us. Instead of guiding and teaching the men we let into our space, we do it for them. We enable bad behavior, we give excuses for why or why not, and we don't let them take responsibility for their mishaps. However, as we grow older, and we start to dig deep into who we are and learn to love ourselves, we begin to analyze what love is and what does love genuinely looks like. We begin to analyze the relationships we are cultivating and aligning them with our new truth. We start to put the pieces together and promote or demote accordingly. Of course, this only happens if you're making a conscious decision to know who you are and what your purpose is.

Every day, I thank God for His mercy on my life because I have not always been the best person to others or myself, for that matter. I thank Him for the desires He's placed in my heart to help others and to become a better person. Nothing or anyone could have filled me up like God. Being a part of a church and around people that teach you the Word really makes a difference. I've always had faith, but to live my life through His eyes, His purpose, by His will is different. We can know all day, but if we don't take action to what He says, then we are no good to others. Faith without works is useless. I like to read the story of David. Not only because he was a great warrior, but also because He was not the type of person we would think Jesus would choose to be a king. He was not perfect by a long shot. He repeatedly sinned, though he was after God's own heart. How many times do we sin and ask for forgiveness? God's love is undeniable. I am living proof of God's undying love. The very fact that I am here and still willing to help those who stepped on me, who left me for dead, who forgot who I was is a miracle. I thank God I don't look like what I've been through and that I've learned to embrace the struggle and to love the struggle because it's through the struggle that God teaches us who we are in Him. Favor is not fair, but it is certainly appreciated.

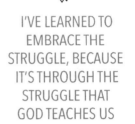

I'VE LEARNED TO EMBRACE THE STRUGGLE, BECAUSE IT'S THROUGH THE STRUGGLE THAT GOD TEACHES US WHO WE ARE IN HIM.

My father lived with me for three years before I realized he could no longer stay in the house alone while my husband and I went to work. Homehealth kept denying him services even though his health was on a downward spiral. Once he fell down the stairs, and his fall punctured a huge hole in the wall. Thankfully he was okay. On different occasions, he fell three times in his bathroom. Other times I had to take him to the hospital whenever his blood pressure was over 180. It didn't matter that I had to wake up for work at 5:30 am or that my daughter had school the next day. I had to be there with him and make sure he was okay. After a while, the nurses and doctors got to know us and so I was able to leave him there alone until he was discharged. It got to the point where I was praying to God for it not to be a weekday when I had to run him to the emergency room because I knew it would be almost impossible to go to work the next morning and also because I would probably still be at work by the time they released him. I prayed, Lord, let it be a weekend. I will never forget on one occasion when he had a bad urinary infection. He had to go to the hospital to have a pick put into his vain so that I could administer medication every day for the next 14 days. I had to learn how to attach the bag so it would drip properly and then once it was done, I had to flush the IV. To do this, I had to be home at certain times because he needed it every 12 hours. Sometimes that meant going to places later or leaving some places earlier to make it on time. In hindsight, it seemed like something very simple to do, until I found myself making adjustments to my own life to care for someone who doesn't even appreciate it. There were many times when the needs of my family were sacrificed due to time spent caring for Papi. None of which he cared about.

My daughter was an awesome helper, though I will never forget the time she asked, "Why does it seem like Abuelo is the kid, and I'm the adult?" I felt her statement in my heart, but I made sure to explain to her the situation. I could not let that teachable moment slip by. I had to acknowledge and accept that my immediate family comes first. And I had to make some changes to my daily routine yet again. Even though I was going through trying to tend to everyone and everything, they (my husband and daughter) were also going through the process second-handedly. Overall, I knew that I was doing some things wrong and that I had to stand up to my father, which meant putting him and his needs on a schedule that accommodated my family. I could no longer make runs to the supermarket or pharmacy three or four times a week. I had to limit the time I spent running around for him and with him so that I could make time for my own family. From that day on, every time I turned down a request, he got angry and began to do things to spite me. For instance, he would refuse to eat dinner even though he was hungry. He also would rather risk falling down the stairs just to make a sandwich rather than eat whatever I had cooked and brought up to his room. His actions and his ingratitude bothered me so much it was reflecting on my health, my job, and schoolwork. As a doctoral student at that time, it was nearly impossible to focus. Lord, was I happy to receive the blessing of church on Sundays!! I needed prayer! I prayed for the Lord to give me strength and wisdom to deal with him and his ways.

Eventually, I realized that I had to continue to do the best that I could without feeling bad, given the fact that he made conscious decisions to go against me. He was trying to manipulate me, and he did so for a good while until I put my foot down. I started by giving him a schedule with a list of errands and tasks. I no longer conformed to his wishes, and it grew a wedge between us. Still, I made sure to be careful to treat him the same way I had been treating him, just with stipulations to preserve my sanity. This time, I would take care to do so more wisely than before. I had to respect the many other hats I wore. Each deserved my time, energy, and love. In all, I was doing the best I could do for Papi, who managed to make me feel less appreciated each time.

It seemed the falls in the house would not cease. Papi fell a few times while I was at work and once in the middle of the night while I was at home. There came a time when I was scared to even walk into his room because of what I would find—him unconscious on the floor or something worse. Luckily, he didn't get hurt too badly from the additional falls, but those falls made me realize he could no longer stay home alone. I devised a plan with his brother in Dominican Republic to see if he could go live there with his family. For many years, Papi had wanted to move back to his home country. Well, if everything worked out, this was his chance, and he didn't need to win the lottery to do so. My uncle moved to a bigger place to accommodate Papi's arrival. I sent the down payment for the new place to help with deposit and other expenses. My father would have his own room and bathroom. My uncle worked mornings, and his wife changed her schedule to work nights. That way, Papi would never be in the house alone. I was so grateful for their willingness to change their lifestyle and accept another person into their family. However, I was skeptical about the money situation because I had to keep in mind that the extra money would suit them very well, and I didn't want that to be a negative factor. Being in a third world country, it is easy for people to take advantage of my dad, especially in his condition.

I bought the ticket and took him shopping for items per his request. He bought so many outfits and shoes. You'd think he was going over to party and find a wife. However, he did nothing but waste time and money. He did not appreciate anyone's efforts to make him as comfortable as possible even though they put him before their own immediate family. It was no surprise to me because I had already lived it for a couple years, but because this was his family and he always made them feel loved by sending them money and caring for them while living in the states, I thought he would behave differently. I guess I figured their dynamic would be different than the way he was with me. But he was a pest there as well. My uncle and his family had a hard time understanding what his expectations were. They ran all his errands, cooked, and basically granted his every want. I had my doubts at first if they were doing all they could, but the stories and the character my father displayed with them was all too familiar. I knew all about those tantrums and the emotional manipulation my uncle had to deal with. Eventually, neither my uncle nor my dad could take him living in the Dominican Republic and he asked to move back. I didn't oppose it; I just told him to give me until the summer so that I could help him find a place to live. I knew I would have more time in the summer because I would have time off, given my employment with the school system. Unfortunately my request was ignored.

Papi bought his flight on his own and was in Miami against my wishes. I was livid because he was calling nonstop from the airport and I was at work. Since he did whatever he wanted to do, I told him he had to handle his own situation at this point. He ended up calling the ambulance due to an elevated blood pressure and was taken to the nearest hospital for treatment. Of course, they called me. I politely told them that he is a grown man and I had no legal rights to him or any of the decisions he made. As I was talking to someone from the hospital, I couldn't believe that he had totally gone against what I said and then tried to have me come "save" him. Before being taken to the hospital, he had even forgotten to claim his baggage. Two days after he's been in the hospital, he called to ask me if I could pick up his luggage??? Ummmmm, NO! He gave me a number and everything.

"If you have the number, why don't you call yourself just like you're calling me"? I asked.

"Well, if you're gonna be that way about it, then I won't ever bother to call you again! And you can just forget I ever existed"! He responded with his usual manipulation.

I said, "Okay, if that's what you want." Then, I hung up. I was appalled at the audacity of him. Here I am, his only daughter, in distress for so many years because my father was not there for me. Yet, later having to care for him despite what my mind told me what my husband told me—that is, don't do It! Ignoring both warnings, I took care of him anyway, overlooking his selfishness and ingratitude. Once again, I found myself FATHERLESS. I got mad at him as well as at myself. I sulked in that pain for a while. Still, in the end, what did I end up doing you may ask? I collaborated with the hospital social worker and gave her all the details she needed to apply for assistance for him to get him into a nursing home or assisted living facility. It worked! She gave me some options. I looked them up online and chose one that I thought would suit his needs. I then got in contact with the representative for the home and gave her all the documents she needed to move forward, Bank statements, and access to his Florida state assistance account. I also answered all kinds of questions regarding his health. Anything she needed, she got, despite Papi's protests that he could make decisions without me and could do things on his own. He was a grown man after all, but not at all able to manage his needs. I then called the airline to get his baggage shipped to his new place (the co-dependence was insane, I know!). When he got to his new place, his bags were there waiting for him. The same bags which he had said, "Fuck the bags! I just won't have shit. I don't care. Don't call then." That was another of his manipulative tantrums to get things his way. To this day, he has yet to say, "thank you." I wonder if he thinks they magically just appeared there. He is truly a piece of work!

There's something about letting go of what you can no longer handle. First you must admit that the thing is beyond your limits and ability. Secondly, you must give yourself space from it. I know both were true for me. That's why I did not rush down to see Papi nor call him after I hung up on him. I knew that I had to move forward in the best way that was good for me, not him. Which is why I took my blessed time in connecting back with him once I knew he was situated. I took care of everything without talking to him directly. I figured that was the Christian thing to do.

THERE'S SOMETHING ABOUT LETTING GO OF WHAT YOU CAN NO LONGER HANDLE. FIRST YOU MUST ADMIT THAT THE THING IS BEYOND YOUR LIMITS AND ABILITY.

I remember telling my boss a little bit about the situation with my dad. The whole scenario floored him. I guess that day I looked stressed out more than usual, prompting him to ask how I am doing. I had to admit

I wasn't okay, but I was maintaining. It felt good to let things out, kind of cathartic. It was also during that time that I remembered the wisdom of my strengthening coach in high school. Whenever you feel like giving up, he said, "On your worst day, you still have to be good enough to win." I deeply believe that. I still live by that principle after all these years.

 In all, I have had some things happen to me that should've taken me out. Yes, from some experiences, I should've died. But I am here and well. And, that's not by accident. Choose to love yourself. Choose to search for your purpose. Choose to set boundaries for those who say they love you. Choose to set the standard.

Chapter 2
Questions

Have you ever developed a strong bond (negative or positive) with a person? How did it make you feel? What did you learn from it?

Discuss a significant person in your life whom didn't make it to your special day (graduation, wedding, an accomplishment). How did that make you feel? Do you think that experience affects decisions you make in your daily life? Why or why not?

Sometimes we do things for people who don't appreciate us. Talk about a time you stopped doing for others who took you for granted. Why should you cultivate your relationship with those people and form a positive bond?

Overall, Chapter Two Reflections

Chapter 3
Making Drug Runs with Mom and Living in My Own Valley

Phenomenal. Amazing. Powerful. Relentless. Forgiving. Beautiful. Free. In many ways, I aspire to be just like her. Her passion and her grit to live a happy life surpasses the peak of the tallest mountain. To this day, my mother remains the most amazing woman I have ever met.

This part of the book is the most emotional for me. You see, for years, I've wanted to tell my mom just how much she means to me. However, until now, I could never quite find the words to describe the immense beast this lady has awakened in me. Let me explain. There was a time growing up where, because of Mami's lifestyle at that time, I went through some unbelievable dramatic events that involved adult-sized dangers no kid should have to face. Yet, it took those shaky times and her own experiences to mold me into the person I am today. Nowadays, in spending time with her, I can't help but be reminded of how special she truly is. Whether we believe it or not, God chose our parents because He knew that together they had the genetic make-up that would form us into exactly who he created us to be long before we were born. It was hard to see it and understand it as a child, but now I am in awe at her strength. I thank God that He touched her and changed her life in such a way that it brought me closer to my destiny and in my relationship with Him because I know it was no one but God who was able to reach deep down into the valley and pull Mami out of her hell. Psalms 23:4 states, "Even though I walk through the valley of the shadow of death, I will fear no evil, for you are with me; your rod and your staff, they comfort me (ESV). With that said, let me begin the story of Mami.

DOWN IN THE VALLEY WITH MAMI

It was the 1980s, and drugs were readily available, even for the poor, which we were. Many of my family members were drug users, and the story was no different for Mami. As I write this chapter, I can remember the smell of drugs burning behind the door of the bathroom. The odor was much like the smell of a freshly opened permanent marker. It was worse when she smoked her drugs, for her breath always smelled like she'd just burned plastic in her mouth or something. Like most of the other addicts in the family, crack cocaine was her choice of drug then. I'm not sure how long Mami was an addict, but I do remember going with her many times to make runs to her dealer. Her rendezvous almost always took place late nights when many other addicts lingered in the dark corners to hide their shame or walked the streets looking for just one more hit before turning in. We lived close to the projects in northwest Miami. The only reason why it wasn't officially called the "projects" was that the development we lived in wasn't government-owned.

It was during this time that Papi was serving time in a Bahamian prison, leaving my mother in charge of every responsibility in caring for my brother and me. Though she received some government assistance, she also worked her butt off to provide for us—at least until the drugs got the upper hand to her health. She was skilled at making much out of the little we had, and my brother and I were happy kids for the most part, but she had started to look so fragile, it was apparent that she was on drugs heavily.

As time progressed, Mami's health began to deteriorate. Mentally, she was still sharp. But the frame of her body told a different story about her overall health. For a woman still in her 30's, Momma looked like she had aged 15 years. She lost so much weight that she was basically skin and bones at one point. I could not help noticing the small burns on the tips of her fingers and her lips. The dark nail polish and lipstick she plastered on her nails and lips were no match for those burns. I got to the point where I could automatically spot them with hardly any effort. Many nights she would put us to bed, and when she thought we were asleep, she would slip away to her dealer. There came a time when I got scared for her safety on our dangerous streets. At 9 or 10 years old, I was faced with a serious dilemma between watching over her or staying with my very young brother during one of her runs. I thought, do I pretend to be asleep and stay home with my brother, or do I get up and make it hard for her to leave the house? I wasn't sure which was worse—going with her to buy drugs or leaving a toddler in the apartment alone. I have a 10-year-old daughter now, and as I write this, I look at her, and I cannot imagine her having to make such a decision.

As a fourth-grader, I was well aware that our streets were not the safest.

Not only that, but I was also totally aware that Mami's addiction was getting out of control. I knew the truth and had known it for some time. I knew that Mami was on drugs, and I knew that my father was locked up in the Bahamas because drugs were found on the ship he worked on. I never really found out if he knew the drugs were there, but more than likely, he knew and had a mission. Like I said, I was not naïve. Although I was Papi's little girl, I knew Papi was no saint.

My mom was an addict for a few years but never neglected her responsibilities. She was what people call a "functional" addict. She went to work, she cared for my brother and me, and made sure we had a roof over our heads and food to eat. As she increased her use, I became quite concerned and feared for her life. Many days I dreamt of horrible scenarios of her dying a horrendous death. Some nights were worse than others as fear had me conjuring up awful possibilities of what could happen to her. For a while, I thought, what if she doesn't come back? What if she gets raped? What if she gets shot? After all, shootings were the norm in the neighborhood. I may have been young, but I knew what happened in those streets. I was born and raised in the neighborhood, and I didn't have to be a rocket scientist to see how dangerous things were on our streets.

As the days turned into weeks and the weeks into months, Momma continued making trips to the dealer, leaving me no choice but to make an executive decision that could negatively impact our household. I decided to leave my baby brother at home alone many nights and make runs with Mami to the dealers. However, before resorting to that, I started waking up whenever I felt her getting ready to creep out of the house in hopes that she would think it was too risky to leave to buy drugs. But she didn't think it was risky at all and went out anyway. I surmised then that the addiction was too strong and championed her better judgment most times. So, I started going on drug runs with her. I remember her pulling up in our old but reliable car to dark places in the corners and alleys of streets. I always made a special effort to try to remember the faces of the dealers or other addicts we would run across because who knows what could transpire. To me, they all looked shady. They were not the kind of people I would want to entrust with my life. For instance, there was one woman that Mami visited frequently. Her name was Keisha. She was always nice to me, though I was sure from her physical appearance and slurred speech that she was as much as an addict as my mother. During Mami's runs to her house, she would stay long enough to smoke crack with Keisha. The funny thing was I always felt at ease at Keisha's. She and my mom would talk while she French-braided my hair. I guess to some extent being there made me feel like I could keep an eye on my mom and knew that as long as she was at Keisha's, she was safe. Plus, anyone wanted to kill her for what-ever reason; they would have to think twice about it since I was there. Now that I'm older, I know that's not the best way to think; but at the time, it seemed like it was the best strategy I could come up with to keep watch over my mother.

Some time passed, and my father was released from prison and came back home. The fights and the arguments between him and Mami were many, and each one equally unbearable. I think what upset him so much was that he knew she had become addicted to crack cocaine while he was gone.

In time, Mami entered a rehabilitation center. She got sober, got a job, and began to stand on her own two feet apart from Papi. She saved money, bought a house, started a business, and worked her tail off to give us a decent life. I cannot put into words how living through the drug addiction with her molded me and shaped me to believe that no matter where I come from and what I've been through, I must take charge of my life and bring a new outlook on life to my generation and those following ahead of me. Generational curses must be broken, and I have set out to do just that for myself, for my siblings, for my daughter, and every generation thereafter.

ALONE IN MY OWN VALLEY OF SEXUAL ABUSE

Growing up in a traditional home in my culture meant that little girls were never to be left alone with males, nor be outside unaccompanied, and they must always come in the house before dark. Also, when wearing a skirt or a dress, girls should wear shorts underneath. I remember having to sit with my legs pressed tightly together. This meant my knees had to touch, or my legs had to be crossed at the ankles. If girls wore shorts, the shorts had to be at least arm's length. Skirts and dresses, on the other hand, had to be just above the knees. That is how things were for me and many other young girls in my neighborhood and my family. My father was a stickler for these rules, and he did not waiver from them because, in his mind, they served to keep me safe from unwarranted advances from males. Trouble was he was not always around to keep me safe or save me from harm.

I was in the fifth grade when my mom finally completed a drug rehabilitation in-house sober living program. I stayed with my dad while she completed the program. I remember being so anxious awaiting her arrival at his house to pick me up and take me to my grandmother's home, where she, my little brother, and I would live together once again. The three of us shared a big bedroom in my grandmother's home. Though her house was large enough to accommodate several other relatives and us, there was absolutely no privacy. We also had little to no say on who could come in and out of the house nor on visitation hours. It was no wonder that family, friends, and neighbors used to come by all the time without warning. Some just to chat, others to stay a night or two as needed. It was not unusual for any of her many children to retreat there when things did not go according to their plans. This happened often. A number of them made pit stops there when life was just not treating them right, and they needed a helping hand. My grandmother was quite generous and could never put her foot down whenever someone was in need. She never closed the door to any of her children. Perhaps one could argue whether that's a good idea or not, but hey, a mother's love, is indisputable. When no one else seems to be there, moms usually won't disappoint, regardless of age.

At any rate, we were excited to be together even if it meant dealing with unexpected company for a while until Mami could afford her own place. As time went on, Mami had begun to steady date one particular man she had met while she was in rehabilitation. He was a recovering alcoholic who had been sober for over 20 years until he relapsed and found himself in rehab. He was a nice-looking, older man who seemed to really love Mami. Sometimes when she went out with her boyfriend, she left us kids home alone with my grandmother. However, grandma was not the best babysitter. She would always go to sleep early because she was still working a full-time job and had to get up early every day.

She worked at the airport and therefore was always up and out of the house in the wee hours of the morning. One night I woke up due to the sound of a commotion outside my bedroom window. It wasn't a loud noise or anything, but it was definitely someone talking. I was so sleepy that I could barely open my eyes. When I inched them open just a little, I saw a shadow. Feeling like I was in a daze, I quickly fell back to sleep. I awakened again. This time, I felt a beard down in my private area. Just remembering the feeling of prickly hairs down in my panties still makes me sick to my stomach. I was so scared, too frightened, to say anything. After a while, I realized the bearded face against my genitals was my uncle.

I was so shocked that I instantly froze. I stayed still and quiet and pretended I was dead asleep. A part of me felt that he would stop if I acted like I was asleep while at the same time having the urge to get up and dart out of the room to tell grandma! Mami! Anybody! I couldn't believe it was happening to me. Unfortunately, I was conscious the whole time the bearded man molested me. Unlike some of my relatives, I wasn't on drugs or under the influence of alcohol to drown out what had just happened to me. I was coherent. I prayed he would stop. After what felt like an eternity, the prickly hairs stopped moving against my genitalia. He hadn't gone any further, and I am so thankful for that!

When he snuck out, I remained motionless. After a while, I curled up in a fetal position and didn't get out of my bed. I wanted to think it was a lie and that it was all just a bad dream. Maybe thinking it was a bad dream would have worked if I hadn't seen my panties on the floor the next morning. It wasn't just a nightmare, it really happened, and the proof was lying there on the floor. What happened really happened.

My uncle had molested me. When that reality set in, I quickly grabbed my panties, put them on, and ran to tell my grandmother. I opened the door to my room, and there she was in her work uniform walking out of her room and talking to herself, as usual, complaining about this and that. I managed to get her attention, and I told her what had happened. In response to my news about her son, she raised her hand at me, and I jumped back. I thought she was going to hit me. She used her pointer finger and firmly told me never to repeat such things. I stared at her in disbelief. She doesn't even believe me, I thought. From what she said, not only did she not believe me, she also didn't want anyone else to know. She made sure to mention that, and she was so distraught that I would accuse her son of molestation that she kept talking about it to herself allll the way to the kitchen. I contemplated telling my mom, but I didn't tell her. I never said anything to anyone for years to come.

For many years I excused my grandmother's response to my pain. I made myself believe that she just didn't know any better. Maybe she's just scared of what my father would do to my uncle if he found out that he had touched his little girl. Regardless of her actual reasons for demanding my silence, our relationship changed forever that day. I remained respectful to her, but I did not see her as my friend or even someone I could trust ever again. When we finally moved out of her house. I saw my grandma less and less, and I was totally fine with that. Using explicit language, she would complain that "now that you're grown, you forget about all your grandma did for you. You have friends and a boyfriend and ya smelling yourself". I paid her no mind. I knew the real reason why I had distanced myself from her.

Have you ever had one of those moments when things are going okay, and then suddenly they change on you? Well, that happened to me years after the incident with my uncle. I had given birth to my first child—my baby girl. By that time, my grandmother had grown frail in strength. She used to ask to watch my baby girl, and I would create a million reasons why I could not bring her over for a visit.

One day, I went to my aunt's house with the baby so she could care for her and I can rest and hopefully catch up on some sleep while I was there. I was a new mom, and sleep was a gift at this point. As I walked into her apartment, there was my grandma who had spent the night. I didn't mind except for the fact that I knew she would probably be yapping away about who did what to her or to someone in the 60s, the 70s, and recount how my grandfather left her to fend for herself with ten kids in the United States. I greeted her with the typical hello and a quick hug and continued to the bedroom to lay the baby down and hopefully take a nap. I don't think I slept at all. I could hear her talking non-stop in the living room. Unable to fall asleep, I sat up straightway when I overheard her bring up the situation I had confided in her years ago! Could she be talking about me? I thought that after all these years, she had probably forgotten about it. As for me, I had already forgiven her for not believing me. After all, I said to myself, she's older now and probably doesn't even remember it. I remember thinking since she re-members, then surely she could have asked me to forgive her for calling me a liar and dismissing my claims. Especially since, to my surprise, my aunt had recently confessed that my uncle had touched her as well. I felt that I had a special bond with my aunt because of it, but I also questioned why she had not spoken up about him. Did she not realize that her silence about his behavior put the other girls in the family at risk of being molested or raped? I'm not sure if she ever told my grandma when she was younger, but I knew that they had had a huge argument about it a couple of years ago. Anyway, I hopped off the bed and moved closer to the door to hear more clearly.

"Cause girls lie all the time, and they don't understand the severity of those lies. How the hell she gonna say that John touched her? I almost slapped her in the mouth."

My blood was boiling. I was so upset! I thought this woman remembered! She remembered every detail from that morning when I ran to her thinking I would get some support. Instead, her response left me feeling like I was the guilty party. I had been a victim twice that day — a victim of abuse and a victim of betrayal. I could not bear to listen any longer. I packed up all of my belongings and was headed out the door. At that moment, my aunt walked in and asked what I was doing. I felt myself tearing up and tried to hold back the tears. "All this time I thought she just didn't remember, and I forgave her for not believing me, only to hear her talking about it now. She knows! And after hearing what he did to you, she still doesn't believe me? Like I'm some girl from the streets that just wants to lie on her son? What would I gain from that? Why would I lie?"

My aunt just looked at me. She tried to make up an excuse about why I should just ignore her, but I could no longer go along with the cover-up. Interestingly, some families believe family ties must not be broken and remain intact at all costs, regardless of what one member does to another. I guessed that's how my aunt felt that day. But I wasn't having it. I got my baby, and I stormed out the door. I didn't utter one word to her or my grandmother. As I stormed out, I imagined they had a conversation about it. I imagined my grandmother continued with the denial because she never spoke about it again, at least not to me. Our relationship would be tainted forever.

Eventually, I would come to forgive my grandmother yet again. Like my aunt, maybe there is a part of me that does not want family ties broken if I can avoid it. The ordeal with my grandmother's denial and demand that I keep silent about her son taught me something valuable. I learned that we must rise above the wrong our families teach us. I genuinely believe in the saying, "when you know better, you do better." It's true. I decided that maybe she just didn't know any better. Perhaps the same thing happened to her when she was younger. After all, she was the only girl and had seven brothers. I will truly never know, but because of this situation, I have never left my daughter over her house or anyone's house until she was old enough to look after herself. Even then, I taught her early on to tell me anytime she did not feel safe around someone. We've even formulated a code word just between us girls.

BEING THE OLDEST: A GIFT AND A CURSE

I love my siblings, but it was not an easy job to lead them. I am the oldest of Mami's three children. Though there are some perks, overall, I feel like I had a lot of pressure on my shoulders. This feeling was especially pressing as we all got older.

When Mami announced she was expecting a baby, I was so excited. I wanted to be the best big sister ever and to practically become his mother from the day he was born. When Mami was thinking of names, I said, "I know what to name him! Kenny!" When Mami asked why I told her it was because Kenny rhymes with Jenny. From the second he was born, I loved him. I changed his diapers, I fed him, and I rocked him to sleep. Mami was so proud of how I was accepting the challenge of being a big sister. The years went by, and of course, my brother went from an adorable baby to a pain in my butt, yet, we loved each other.

Whenever I wanted to go out with my friends, I had to take my brother. I thought it was so unfair, but I wanted to go. So, at times, there I was at the movies with a 7-year-old who threw tantrums whenever he didn't get what he wanted. "I don't want to watch that movie! I want popcorn and candy and a drink."

To make matters worse, I only had enough money for the movie tickets, my father would not give any extra because we just did not have money like that, but he didn't understand that at his age. He would continue screaming for all the goodies in the concession stand. I would have to drag him through the crowd of people as he kicked and cried in resistance. I had had enough on one movie outing and decided that from that point forward, I would think twice about asking for permission to go anywhere!

From what I can remember, there was only one time when my brother and I were separated, but not by choice. When Mami went to rehab, she was allowed to take only one of her children with her, so she took him. I had to stay with Papi until she recovered. As I mentioned previously, we were able to come together again as a family when she was released from rehab, and I was happy when that day came. My brother is now 27 years old, and yet I still feel a keen sense of responsibility for him. I feel obligated to help him navigate life. To this day, I keep trying to help him find his way. I feel responsible for his success or demise. I pray for him fervently, and I pray that God continues to build a hedge around him. Admittedly, I have a soft spot for him, not only because he's my brother, but also because I think that he's always wanted to be my protector. You see, he watched me go through one of the hardest times of my life. When I was molested, he experienced my hurt and pain firsthand. Because I was upset that my grandma dismissed my plea for help when I told her my uncle molested me, I feel that I mistreated my brother many times because of the anger I had built within. He was so young and helpless to the fact that I had been violated and had no idea that this had even occurred. To this day, I don't believe he knows (he will after reading this).

As an adult, looking back at this situation was pretty tough, but even worse was giving my siblings (my sister was born by this time), a dreadful memory they probably will never forget and one I never saw coming. In high school, I was in a relationship that became mentally and emotionally taxing. As time went on, it became physically violent. In the next chapter, I go into detail, but right now, as it pertains to my brother, I sense he's kind of hard on himself for not knowing what to do on that dreadful day. Even though it is not something we talk about at all. To this day, I have always wanted him to know that there was nothing he could do; Nothing at all. And in actuality, I am glad things turned out the way they did and no one else was physically hurt. I regret he had to see it all. It may be something etched into his mind forever. As I look back on things, I can't help thinking that maybe we should have talked about it so that if I can answer any questions or ease any feelings about that day, I could do it and release those concerns away for good.

When this situation occurred, my brother was about 10. Being so young to do anything to stop this grown man from hurting his big sister could have taken a negative effect on him. This is why I suggest to you, dear reader, do not delay another day to have important discussions with your family members. The hurt may not go away by itself, you know? Talk it out. You'll be glad you did. This is the only thing I would change about caring for my younger sibling that I talk things out with them to help prevent matters that can grow into adulthood and create a false sense of living. We don't have to hide behind our truths. Our truths will set us free and will help us maneuver life a little differently as we see other people and feel compassion toward them because we have lived through some things ourselves.

My sister, the youngest one in the family, came along almost 14 years after my own birth. She's a gem. Growing up, she was always so sickly (she still is), but she's learned how to be a little more cautious. I cared for her as I did my brother. I bathed her, combed and braided her hair, and dressed her up like she was my little human doll. Small and fragile, she was the cutest baby ever. Not too many years after her birth, I had a driver's license and a car. My days began with waking everybody up and getting them ready for school. I would drop them off at school sometimes and then head to Miami Southridge High. At other times, Mami would drop them off in the morning, and I would pick them up after track practice. With partly raising my siblings, going to school, and participating in track, I had a busy life! Aside from everything else, I was a high schooler trying to get a scholarship to run track at somebody's university. Nevertheless, I managed to take care of the household while my mother worked her butt off to provide. She did an excellent job being a provider though we missed her terribly.

During my senior year in high school, things began looking up for me. I won a scholarship to Alabama State University, home of the Mighty Marching Hornets. It was an out-of-state school, and I feared leaving my house, not because of the distance, but because I was not sure how Mami would fend without my help. Not surprisingly, Mami did not hesitate a second in letting me go. She practically pushed me out of the house! She was so proud. As for the finances it would take to keep me in university, she said she'd figure it out somehow. My scholarship only paid for tuition. What a mom!

I missed being home, even though I came back for the major breaks. I was still missing huge chunks of what was going on while I was away. One awesome memory I have when coming home was finding that my brother always stayed up waiting for my car to pull up into the driveway. He would even grab my luggage out of the vehicle. I've always known he loved me and admired me even though he never verbalized it much at all. I often think about the many times he did that. It didn't matter what time I pulled up; he would be waiting. That meant the world to me.

Both of my siblings mean so much to me. These days I find myself looking up to them, for they have overcome obstacles of their own. I love them both for their own character and for the special memories I have shared with each of them separately and together. But mostly, I owe them for helping me become the responsible person I have become today even when I have fallen short of being an exemplary big sister.

THE FACE OF DOMESTIC VIOLENCE

The National Coalition Against Domestic Violence (NCADV) reports that in the state of Florida, 1 in 3 women have experienced physical abuse by an intimate partner. At one time, I was one of those women. I was in high school and living my best days. I was on the track team, cross country team, and basketball team. I loved taking weight training and hanging out with my friends. Just like most young athletes, I was popular because I was involved in school sports. During my junior year, I met a guy that had graduated a year or two before. I was fond of him and we started dating. I thought he was so cool. He was well known and very stylish and had a personality that everyone gravitated toward. He would come to track practices sometimes, and then we'd leave together. We spent a lot of time together.

After dating for some time, he became possessive. Not being as wise as I am today, I gave him the benefit of the doubt and actually thought that his aggression was cute. He would say things like, "Wear your jacket around your waist so your butt won't show." I laughed it off. "Boy, you crazy." Except he didn't laugh in return. So, I dutifully put it around my waist and thought it was a little weird but didn't think much of it. I thought he was just that into me. How naive was I? I took care of him as I did with my siblings. For instance, if he were hungry, I'd feed him like I would my siblings. When his car was messed up, I lent him mine. If Mami knew, she would have killed me. I reasoned that since he lived close to my house and was within walking distance, I would not need the car unless I had track practice. When I did have practice, he would sometimes come and watch. He was at all track meets supporting me. Or so I thought. It was more like he had me under surveillance. For a while, he was very sweet and nice to me. He only showed indifference to me whenever his friends or cousin was around. But I didn't pay it that much attention.

Close to where we lived was an elementary school with an adjacent park where the city often held little league football, intramural football, baseball, and softball games. He had joined one of the intramural teams and played football there often. One evening I came to watch him play. He was upset about something, although I cannot remember what it was. At any rate, he took his anger out on me. I decided it was time for me to walk away because there were a lot of people there and he began to get loud. I didn't want to be embarrassed nor cause a scene. However, he came after me. I told him I would rather leave and go home, but he grabbed me, shoved me on the ground, and told me that I was going to stay until he was ready to go. For what seemed longer than a minute, I just stayed on the ground in shock with panic rising. I didn't know what to do. Was I really going through this? I was so embarrassed. I felt small. I had never felt so small in my life. At that point, I knew I had to get away from him and put an end to this toxic relationship. I got up to walk away while his friends held him back. Luckily his friends succeeded in talking some sense into him, and I was able to get home that night without another confrontation. I didn't tell my mom or anyone else about what had just happened to me. I tried to erase it from my memory, but of course, that didn't happen. It's been almost

20 years, and I still remember exactly how I felt that night. Even after what had happened that night, he came to my house and knocked on my bedroom window. I lifted the window to tell him it was over and that I couldn't forgive him for what he had done. He said he was sorry and that he wouldn't do it again. I told him I had to go to bed and he should not come to my house again.

What followed after that night was a nightmare. He began stalking me. He came by all the time, whether I was home or not. He would even sit in a car that we kept parked in our driveway just to watch for me. Sometimes he would just sit outside of my house to wait for me to arrive. Eventually, he convinced that he was really sorry and all he wanted to do was make it up to me. He said he wouldn't stop coming by until I let him make it up to me and that if I still didn't want to be with him after that, then he'll accept it. Naïve me, let him back into my life. Everything seemed okay for a while until the inevitable happened again. After we had gotten into an argument, he put his hands on me and verbally abused me. I decided that I will not forgive him this time and I called the police on him because he refused to leave my house. When the police came, they let him know that he was trespassing and made him leave.

I was relieved for the moment, but I knew that he would be back eventually. I was right. He kept coming by the house and riding by in different cars to see if I was home. That same week, I decided I had to tell my mom. We filed a restraining order against him. I remember wishing my dad was in the picture at this point. Had he been there, maybe this wouldn't have happened to me. Perhaps he would've taught me the signs of an abusive man. Maybe his very presence would've made this guy think twice before he messed with his little girl.

In retrospect, as I recall this incident of domestic violence, I realize that we all go through things for various reasons. I have a sister, a daughter, and female students whom I have taught over the years and have shared warning signs of domestic violence. As a woman, it is my belief that my journey is not just for me. God intends us to speak to others and to

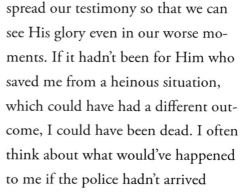

GOD INTENDS US TO SPEAK TO OTHERS AND TO SPREAD OUR TESTIMONY SO THAT WE CAN SEE HIS GLORY EVEN IN OUR WORSE MOMENTS.

spread our testimony so that we can see His glory even in our worse moments. If it hadn't been for Him who saved me from a heinous situation, which could have had a different outcome, I could have been dead. I often think about what would've happened to me if the police hadn't arrived

when they did. I know that God was there with me. In essence, your story is not your story; you're just a vessel. It's His story, and He wants it told everywhere possible, to the world. Even though I can look back at this situation today and see it from a positive perspective, I remember the pain I endured and the dark cloud that followed me constantly in and out of school. Sadly for me, everyone at school knew what had happened. I was so embarrassed and ashamed. My track coach tried to give me some advice. I couldn't believe that even he knew. I couldn't hide my shame anywhere. Everyone knew that something horrible had happened to me on that day when I decided not to let him in my house, and he decided to break in. Everyone also seemed to be the narrator of my story and had their own rendition of what actually took place. The next paragraph will depict step by step the worse horror yet in dealing with this monster that I just couldn't hide from.

One Saturday afternoon, I was home with my siblings. My mom worked tirelessly, so as the oldest, I would be in charge whenever she was gone. She had left the house only about an hour or so when I heard a knock on the door. At this point, I was accustomed to being on edge. I was so scared for my life day in and day out; anything frightened me. I heard the knock again, and immediately my heart dropped. I knew it was him. I urged my siblings to be quiet and moved them into my mom's room. I don't know why I thought it was the most secure room in the house. We locked ourselves in there as I spoke to the police on the phone. I explained that I had a restraining order on this person and that he was knocking on my door, yelling for me to open it. Despite my yelling back about the police coming, he refused to leave. Before I knew it, I heard a window break. Still on the phone, I told the police he was trying to get into the house and that I had heard something break, probably the window. Somehow he got in, came to my mother's room and broke down the door. He grabbed me, causing me to drop the phone while he dragged me out of the room. I fought to get him off me. My main concern was to get him outside and away from my brother and sister. Seeing my car keys, he grabbed them while pushing me outside at the same time. Next thing I knew, we were squared up on my front lawn. I see my brother standing at the front door, and I remember yelling for him to go inside. I had no idea where my little sister was. I remember throwing some blows and him just trying to hit me back and wanting me to get in the car. Finally, I heard sirens of police cars, but they sounded far too away to save me now. I could see my brother had picked up the phone and was probably still speaking with a dispatcher. I also saw my sister standing next to him. So many thoughts ran through my head a million miles per second. Finally, what seemed like forever, I thought, 'Right on freaking time!!'

Police cars sped down my street! Some stopped right in front of my house and others blocking off the street on both ends. My assailant fled on foot down the street and cut in between houses through the yard. One police car followed him, and the other stayed with me. We were all outside at this point... my brother, my sister, and I with police. I had to stand there and explain what had happened and who he was as my little sister, who was now in my arms, crying uncontrollably. I recounted the entire story to the authorities giving the complete background information. They blockaded the streets around my home, but it seemed he had escaped. I was devastated.

After some time, I decided to go back into the house, put on some shoes, get everyone in my car, and leave. As I put on my shoes, I asked my brother to get shoes for my sister. He went into my room to look in the closet. Low and behold, the monster was hiding in my closet! My brother ran outside and told police that he thinks he's hiding in my closet! They rushed in and forced him out of the closet! They struggled to cuff him as he vigorously resisted the arrest. He was pissed off and cussed out the police and kept threatening to come back. He looked at me in the eyes and told me that he won't be in jail long and that he'll be back. I just stared at him.

The next time I saw him was in court. He was sentenced to two years in jail. He looked different. Later on, I heard he had suffered a stroke during his time in jail awaiting trial. Meanwhile, everyone knew him at my school and around the neighborhood, so there wasn't a place I went where I did not feel like someone was whispering about me or the situation soon as they would see me. I don't know why, but for some reason, I felt bad for him. He had never been in trouble with the law before. I found myself feeling guilty. How is it possible to feel guilty for the aggressor? I felt that I was suffering in spite of him being the one in jail. I felt that I was carrying a huge burden and a sign on my forehead that said "victim." I felt that I could have avoided this situation if I had just been smarter. If only I had recognized the signs sooner and listened to my inner voice. I felt that I had put my siblings in danger and that things could have unfolded badly. I felt like I couldn't forgive myself for being naïve and stupid. I felt so guilty.

My sister, whom I shared my bedroom with, would have nightmares since that day. For a while, she would stand at the door of our room and point at the closet, thinking he was still hiding in there. For a while, she wouldn't come in. It broke my heart every time. To soothe her, I would open the closet and say, "See, nothing. You can come with me. It's safe." I would smile and hold my arms out, but then she'd walk away. Every time she walked away, I would bury my face in my pillow and cry. I was lying to her, I thought. I couldn't keep her safe. I had failed as a big sister. I failed as a protector. I internalized so many different feelings and emotions, but I had no choice but to get up every day and keep going. I wanted to put it all behind me. As for my brother, I don't remember him saying much about the situation, but I always felt like he wished he would've done more to help during the altercation. He never spoke much about it, but I knew it would be a while before we were over it and back to normal.

After that, Mami took precautions by putting iron bars on all the windows of the house. Every window, every sliding door, and every back door was also barred. I knew Mami felt angry and upset that I had to go through that situation, and in hindsight, she probably also felt guilty that she worked so much that she didn't see this coming. I knew she was upset that she wasn't there.

Chapter 3
Questions

Discuss a time when you felt responsible to "save" or protect someone. How did you feel?

At any point in your life, did someone violate you in any way? If yes, did you tell someone? If not, do you wish you had spoken up?

I saw a need to break the generational curses in my family, one being molestation. Do you have any generational curses in your family? If yes, what steps have you taken to break the cycle?

Taking into account of hurtful situations in your life, what have you done to heal from those issues?

Overall, Chapter Three Reflections

Chapter 4
Sacrifices and Goals

I think God gave me the perfect parents. He strategically placed me with people who always carried that fight in them, you know? I'm talking about the fight of work and survivorship! That third world country fight with true grit! That "make a dollar out of fifteen cents fight!

I also thank God for allowing me to be born to a praying mother and grandmother. Even though I am no longer a member of a Catholic church, I grew up in Catholicism among other faithful Catholics, like my grandmother who kept candles lit for every saint, every week. As a woman of faith, my mom instilled in me a spirit of perseverance and determination. I don't think Mami ever knew how to guide me to success the "American" way or when exactly to tell me what I needed to do to become successful. Yet, she just knew that I would be. In a weird way, I felt that she lived vicariously through me. She wanted me to go out and explore the world beyond the streets which is why she never sheltered me from life and its devilish ways or the way it can suck you into darkness. She let me explore and be free. In many ways, I knew she trusted me. Even more importantly, I knew she had believed that she had raised me well. She trusted my judgment and my discernment. It came as no real surprise, then, that when I told her I was going to Alabama for college, she was nothing short of cloud nine happy. However, that was our rendition to the beginning of the "American" way to success, and I'd have to figure that one out on my own. From the news, she basically began kicking me out the house! To this day, I am not sure how to take that, but off to college I went on a track and field scholarship!

Growing up I was always athletic. I was quick on my feet and I was a slim little thing just running and playing in our neighborhood streets with my cousins. My cousins and I used to play football outside many days, and I was always a top recruit. Even though I couldn't catch well, if I got the ball, no one could catch me. Isn't that like God? He puts the ball in our hands and watches what we will do with it knowing He has already given us the tools to maneuver it the way needed. He leaves the manual labor up to us to fulfill His will.

I would get handed the ball, then like a bullet, I would zoom by my opponents. I probably should've joined a track club, but my family wasn't really into putting their kids in sports. Or, maybe intuitively, I knew they just couldn't afford it. At the same time, they worked so much, they probably never had the time to get me into a club, much less keep up with a practice and competition schedule. It seemed that back then, everyone worked hard, long hours. Still, there was just never enough time or money. Again, this is the legacy they left me: work hard. It will pay off later on.

Mami pushed education more than anything else. I was a straight-A student throughout elementary and middle school. In high school, I earned some B's and a few Cs. High school was also where I was introduced to Weight Training and took it as an elective. I loved it. I loved to compete against others and I had an athletic build for the class. The weight training coach thought I was a "Burley girl." Everyone knew what a Burley girl was! Coach Burley coached Cross Country and Track and Field for many years and won many championships. He's a legend in South Florida. He was like a father to the girls on his team. He went above and beyond his duty as a coach for each one of them. I wasn't a "Burley girl" at the time, but it didn't take much time to become one. I was far from the fastest or quickest girl on the team. I didn't know where I fit in at all. I had never been a part of an organized sports team before. Many of the other girls had been running since the time they learned how to walk! I was so impressed with all of the talent on the track team. Even though I was not intimidated, I thought that maybe I'd be better cheering them on! They were good and I was just happy to be around so much talent. Upon joining the team, I was determined to give my best at all the times. Coach Burley wouldn't have it any other way anyway. Starting out, I wasn't particularly great at any one event, so I tried many. I got a little smart and decided that I would stick to the pole vault. There weren't many girls that were brave enough to jump in the air with only a stick that you're supposed to bend so it'll fling you over the bar (that's for crazy folks, right?). I wasn't scared, but most importantly, I wanted to be an integral piece of the puzzle for my team to help them win. I wasn't that good at first, but I became more comfortable with it in due time. The summer after I started vaulting, my coach registered me in a pole vault camp at the University of Miami, where I was coached by the professionals and collegiate pole vaulters. I thoroughly enjoyed every bit of it. I loved vaulting even more after that training because I understood the strength and the technique it took to be good at it. However, it is the most challenging and equally danger- ous event on the track.

The following season I improved a whole three feet. That's when I knew that the training worked! I qualified to participate in the state of Florida track & field meet that year. I was ecstatic. I was by far not the best in the state of Florida, but it was enough to at least give me a chance to score points for my team at the state level and help clench a state title. That day in 2002, I did not perform my best, yet I felt so blessed to be in the building. Still, I could not shake the feeling that I let the team down. You see, every point mattered, especially since we were in a neck-to-neck race with rival Miami Northwestern High School. At the end of the night, when the announcer claimed second place to Miami Northwestern High School, we screamed, yelled, and furiously jumped up and down because we knew that meant we were NUMBER 1! That was an experience of a lifetime! I will never forget it.

BECOMING A DISCIPLE OF DISCIPLINE

To many people, it was crazy that I would do such an event like the pole vault in the first place because I had a coach who had no sub- stantial experience in coaching vaulters. Secondly, the track where we practiced had no pit for vaulting. I saw these issues simply as barriers I would have to overcome. My parents taught me that excuses just don't exist. You're going to set out a goal and figure it out, or you're not. That behavior went unsaid. It was what I witnessed from my parents, day in and day out. They had to provide, and "I don't know" or "I don't have it" never gave results. With that said, I had to figure out how to get better despite having a coach who wasn't an expert with such a technical event.

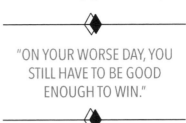

"ON YOUR WORSE DAY, YOU STILL HAVE TO BE GOOD ENOUGH TO WIN."

However, coach never left me hanging. He found a way to get me to a pit and found people who can teach me more than he could in that area. My coach did the next best thing. He devised a plan that would help me get bigger, faster, and stronger. I ran and drilled with the hurdlers. The stride of a hurdler had to be controlled and precise, just like that of a vaulter's.

Additionally, I lifted heavy weights to withstand the pressure of a bending the pole and to have enough upper body strength to invert my entire body up and over the bar. Also, my coach agreed to dedicate one day of the practice week to take me and another teammate to a different track where there was a pit for us to practice. I would watch videos and read the manual of Bill Falk, a pole vault legend and the founder of the training I attended in the summers.

I practiced in phases. I would try to perfect each phase of the run, then the beginning phases of planting the pole, and lastly, the phases of going up in the air. I would envision myself doing each phase with perfection. Just like the pros did it. Visualizing was a massive part of the process for me. Back then, I did not know how much visualizing what I wanted to achieve and where I wanted to be would be such an essential part of my life later on as an adult. One thing I can say about sports is that it entails being disciplined and it spills over into adulthood. It helps children to become self-controlled and it instills a sense of enthusiasm to be better and more well-rounded socially, emotionally, mentally, and physically. Furthermore, the coaches, the camaraderie among peers, and the competitions teach children valuable lessons that they will come to cherish as well as implement throughout their lives. My sweat paid off my senior year at the state championship when I was able to qualify and partake in our championship win. I did not feel as though I did my best, but my team still won, and I cherish that win in my heart! Many things did not go as planned that day, but as my high school weight training coach would say, "On your worse day, you still have to be good enough to win." It is true. In life, though every day may not be the best, you must still get through it the best way you know-how. Meditate, assess the day, and make it better tomorrow. In my case, on days where I didn't perform my best, I learned that I could still be valuable by cheering on my teammates and helping wherever I can to help them perform their best. When you do this, you win even when you 'lost.' Remember this, the making of your character is developed in the losses, not just the wins. Why? Because it takes character to lose and still act like a winner. The key is to never give up!

Discipline and hard work paid off, even more, when I decided to attend Alabama State University (THEEEEE BEST HBCU). It was so far from home and definitely a culture shock, for I was a city girl, born and raised in Miami, moving to country ol' Montgomery, Alabama. I could only imagine the change of environment that was ahead for this city girl. With a push from Mami, coupled with own excitement to experience the world, I enrolled in the school. I hadn't quite envisioned myself in college until my senior year in high school. As I went through the admission process, I kind of doubted my success in such an environment. Quite honestly, I had started to feel anxious and lost. No one in my family had really gone to college and I had no one to guide me through the process. I had a cousin at a local community college in Miami, but no one else that I knew personally had gone to college.

Navigating college life was not easy, and there were many times when I felt confused. I didn't know much about financial aid or what my major would be. Frankly, I hadn't thought about what I wanted to study or become. I wasn't adequately prepared or had the slightest clue at how many different professions there were in the world to even choose what I can aspire to be. All I knew was that I was supposed to graduate high school, go to college, graduate with a degree, and start my career. But what career? How I would accomplish each step to graduating from college? What will become of it all was up to me to figure out, and yet I didn't know where to start. I made so many mistakes throughout my college career. I chose a major, took classes focusing on it, then changed majors and then took more classes only to realize I needed to change my major again because I didn't like the one I had chosen last either. I went from undecided to History to Biology and finally Mass Media Communications, which I was not sure I wanted to have a career in at the end of it all.

I finally graduated with a degree and felt like just maybe that was the right path for me. However, I probably didn't pursue it as tough as I should've once out of school, but I was glad to be done with school. I was ready to move back to Miami, and well, in that field, staying in

Alabama would've probably been the smarter thing to do because it was a much smaller market, and I would be able to navigate through the channels faster. I was already a minority as a Hispanic female in Montgomery, so that would've worked in my favor, I'm sure. However, I was done with Montgomery and was ready for a change in scenery.

Moving back to my hometown was exciting. It was a new journey. I had left to step into the unknown as a little girl with hopes and dreams of nothing but being successful and making Mami proud. Five years later, I returned as a woman with a degree and a new outlook on life. I had many "aha" moments while in college, which helped me understand why Mami did certain things that, as a child and later as a teenager, I just didn't get. But, now that I was an adult, it all started to magically make sense. I began to appreciate her struggle to pay bills, to work, and to help others even if it meant she had to rob Peter to pay Paul. It took me a while to get that one until I had to simultaneously pay the light bill and the gas with a paycheck that wasn't enough to pay both. I had to ask myself, which one would get cut off first to figure out which one needed to be paid first or to figure out how long I have before the lights actually get cut off?

Moving back home was quite the experience. I was used to having my own space even though I had the best roommate ever. She and I remained best friends after graduating. I was sleeping on my Mami's couch, and all my belongings were in boxes. I was so out of place. I felt dislocated. That was my life for a few months as I interned at "CBS 4 Miami". I hoped to get hired afterwards, but there were no openings and honestly, I was barely noticed there though I did everything asked of me and more. At the end of my internship, I got desperate for a job and decided I would go into education. I became a substitute teacher at Miami-Dade Public Schools. The pay wasn't the best, but it was more than I had at the time, and it was experience under my belt. To my surprise, I liked being in the classroom, and so I set out to become certified as an educator. I returned to my high school alma mater and subbed in mostly special education classes. I had a special place in my heart for kids with special needs and quite frankly, I enjoyed helping them. I also liked the hands-on life skills that I provided those kids. They touched my heart in a unique way, and within months I decided I was going back to school to earn a master's degree in Special Education. I didn't want to go back on a campus, so I applied to the University of Phoenix and began my studies online.

It would still be a while before I graduated and obtain employment as a special education teacher. Also, I was quite cognizant that my student loans were through the roof and needed to be paid off. My best friend was kind of in a rut after college as well, and jobs were just not easy to come by. I remember even applying at McDonald's just to make some money for the time being and was denied employment because I was overqualified. It was a tough time for me. I was a recent college graduate with no money and no job with student loan collectors calling me. My bestie and I vented to each other often, and then we both came up with the same conclusion. Join the army! At the time, they were offering to pay for college and had a huge signing bonus. It seemed like it was a great idea. We went to a recruiting station to get more information. We already had degrees, so we wouldn't start at the bottom of the totem pole. That was a great thing. Because we had a bachelor's degree already, we had the option to go the officer training route. We chose instead to go the noncommissioned officer route, which I regretted later. I should have made a better decision, but I was not as informed as I should've been. I took it as a lesson learned! The truth is, I shouldn't have rushed through that decision and that having the necessary pieces of information is key to your success, not just in the present, but even for later in life. Everything we do now affects our lives later.

We took the ASVAB and before we knew it, we were signing up. It happened fast. There was no turning back. It was scary to go into the unknown, but at the same time, I was an athlete, my best friend was an athlete, so boot camp wasn't something we worried about. For me, I feared getting deployed. I wasn't sure what to expect. I watched videos on YouTube, and some were horror stories. However, once I got there, I realized that the toughest thing was getting over the feeling of being lonely dealing with being away from family, and, of course, following the rules and orders of drill sergeants. My husband, who was my boyfriend then, was against me joining the military, but he supported me. Coincidentally, I signed my contract on September 11, a date I will never forget and a day the world commemorates. In a weird way, I felt proud about that. I felt courageous. I felt like I was doing my part to give back to my birth country.

Boot camp was in Fort Leonardwood, Missouri, and it was gruesome to say the least. Many times, I wished I was home. It was freezing cold! The roads were icy and muddy, and snow was everywhere most days. We had to march in all weather conditions. Boot camp was my first time experiencing the snow, and there I was, hating it because I had to stand in it for hours in formation while the drill sergeants sat in their cars with the heat on. I thought I was going to freeze to death. Not only were the temperatures low, the wind was blowing tears right out of my eyes before I can even wink. It felt like the wind was cutting my face. I hated the weather there so much. To this day, I still cringe thinking about it and I can feel the coldness in my bones.

Nevertheless, I rose to the occasion quickly. I stood there and took orders from the drill sergeants as they tried to break us down mentally and physically. I could've exercised all day rather than be in the cold. However, something told me that was part of their plan. Either way, I chose to be there and now I had to suck it up!

I became leader of my platoon. It made me stronger, but not by choice. Every time someone in my squad gave up, did the wrong thing or gave an incorrect answer, I paid for it because, as a leader, I had failed them if what they were doing was not right 100 percent of the time. This meant I had to stay up after hours with soldiers on my squad that were still trying to learn the Soldier's Creed and the three general orders. If they couldn't finish their push-ups or sit-ups, I had to make up the difference. It was my duty to lead and to answer for them. I had to make our Platoon Sergeant look good by having our squad on point! One good thing did come from being leader—I was ripped! I had abs and guns! I was also the champion at combative, intimidating the other females. Honestly, I was probably the scrawniest person there. But I was strong and ended up combating a few of the guys similar in size to myself after I had beaten all the girls. I was strong and I felt strong mentally, emotionally, and physically. And of course, I wasn't going down without a fight due to my competitive nature. That was probably the best shape I'd ever been in my life. I came home weighing 120 pounds, solid.

Joining the track team in high school, going out of state for college, and becoming a United States Army soldier all have a few things in common. They all took discipline, courage, perseverance, and action. I saw each endeavor to the end. When I returned home from basic training, I knew at that moment that I could do anything! I learned that taking risks is a huge factor of life. You see, all of these endeavors were steppingstones to the next big thing. I have yet to "arrive." I learned that in each phase of life, there were lessons that I had to take with me into the next journey. The discipline my parents gave me prepared me for track which in return got me a scholarship. The determination my coaches instilled in me to win and compete, prepared me mentally and physically for the army. Graduating from basic training gave me the confidence that I can achieve anything I set out to do. So don't worry about where you are right now. Instead, be conscious of it and ask God, "What is it that you want me to learn in this season?" Learn the lesson, take risks, and keep moving. Everything you want is on the other side of comfort. And God will get His glory by making you uncomfortable until He has you exactly where He wants you. That's when you'll elevate.

Chapter 4
Questions

Discuss the goals you had as a child and the plan you made to achieve them? Who served as a role model (or someone you looked up to) that helped you achieve those goals?

What are some things you heard as a child or young adult that you did not understand then, but totally understand now?

In this chapter, I speak about joining the army. I feel that I should've been more informed before jumping in. At what point in your life did you jump into a situation or a make a decision with minimal information? Was it worth it? Why or why not?

Name an accomplishment(s) that made you feel so proud and like you can conquer any goal you set. What kind of attitude did you have to possess to achieve this goal?

Overall, Chapter Four Reflections

Chapter 5
Overcoming the Triple Threat

All things, not some things, but all things work together
for good for those who love the Lord
- Romans 8:28

GROWING UP POOR

I grew up knowing that I was born in Miami, Florida, and was equally proud of being a Latina. Due in large part to my ancestors, I carried Dominican roots deep in my blood and was never ashamed to own my ethnic heritage regardless of where I was or who was around me.

To this day, I remember the many places where my family and I lived that were rich in culture and short on resources, including North Miami, Wynwood, Overtown, and even Little Haiti. Socioeconomically, they were all depressed areas. Some people may even name them among some of America's worst ghettoes. For me as a kid, it seemed that in all those neighborhoods, Blacks and Hispanics—regardless of which ethnic group were the majority in the area—were in a struggle together to survive poverty as best we could. We endured the kind of poverty that was not going away overnight. No, the struggle we endured was persistent. It was with us every day and had the power to lock us into constraints such as where we could live, how often we could purchase necessities and even the quality of medical care we could have.

An interesting commonality among those who lived in the aforementioned neighborhoods is that everyone was on government assistance. Not one family was able to get by without it. Something else I held in common with the other neighborhood kids was that I was often made to go to the corner supermarket with food stamps in hand. Back then, we were issued food stamps that were different colors and came in a little booklet the size of a checkbook. The funny thing is, we were all happy and excited to have them. You would be hard-pressed to find one family that was ashamed of being on government assistance. Hell, we thought everybody was! It's almost like we felt bad for those that weren't. If it was discovered that if a family were denied government assistance for some reason, we would point them to the expert in the neighborhood for advice to ensure when they applied again, they get approved! We knew that no family in that area could survive without assistance. No matter which depressed area of Miami one lived, there was this one prevailing principle that everybody abided by. Life is what you make it, and if government assistance were a part of your life, then make them work for you.

There seems to be a positive connotation on being from "the hood" nowadays. I just want to make it known that just because I was able to rise above poverty, it doesn't mean that I enjoyed "the hood." Sure, there are positive things I remember like ice cream trucks coming by and being able to play in the streets with the neighborhood kids, but there were also very scary moments. I do not want anyone to get the wrong idea that living in poverty was 'fun.' Let the record state that growing up poor is a struggle for kids. As I mentioned before, limited resources leave limited choices for families, and mine was no different. And, I dare say that Mami's addiction may have been predicated on the fact that she was depressed about not being able to care for her babies in ways she saw other families care for their children. That in those very streets I grew up in, she was able to find comfort inhaling the crack sold on every corner. What else was she was to do to escape the realities and pain of poverty? What she could do for us was determined by the amount of money she could make as a Latina in America with limited education and limited resources.

FACING LIFE IN AMERICA AS A LATINA

We may sing that America is the land of the free and home of the brave, but in actuality, nothing is free in this country. The American dream costs, dear friends. And it's not cheap either. Indeed, one must work tirelessly to achieve that two-car garage house with a picket fence, boat, sufficient finances for a college education for the children, and all other great things. In my case, fulfilling the American dream would have been very difficult had I not been educated by the rude awakening of genderism and racism in this country. Both were hard teachers, but necessary to achieve my goals as a Latina in America.

Being raised by immigrant parents and feeling the wrath of social injustice in America, as well as sexual abuse in my own home, taught me well. I learned from a young age that I had to work ten times harder than, say, the majority race, if I was going to be taken seriously. That work ethic was instilled in me from a young age, and it's something to which I still adhere. My parents kept me on a strict schedule. I had to

clean, cook, do homework, and think about my future all at the same
time. Then when my brother was born, my responsibilities increased to
having to take care of him. I didn't have a choice. I couldn't say, "that's
your kid, not mine," even though I wanted to belch that from the
bottom of my stomach many times whenever he got on my nerves. As I
admitted, my family depended on government assistance, but they also
worked hard. This I remember for most of my life. We were no strang-
ers to financial struggles.

Today, as an educator and mother, I try to instill the crucial ethic of
hard work in to my daughter, just as Mami did for me. Genetically,
my daughter is a mixture of Hispanic and African American. As you
might imagine, her ethnic blend precludes some people in this country
from considering the content of her character rather than her genes.
This is even more reason why I want her to understand that working
for what she wants is crucial, for nothing will be handed to her. That
is why I put her on the same kind of strict schedule my own parents
kept me on when I was growing up. I want her focused and disciplined
to handle the challenges that lie ahead. I want her to learn early how
to be an overcomer of any challenge or barrier that may be in her way
simply because of who she is. In doing this, as an adult, I also have to
be mindful not to instill some toxic behaviors that I grew up with. As
a parent or role model, how do you decipher what is toxic and what is
not, and how do you ensure that it is not passed on from generation to
generation? The most important thing is to recognize those behaviors.
Reflect on how you grew up. What did you like or not like about what
people said to you and how they treated you? That is the first step. Then
finding a way to heal from those toxicities, whether it be therapy or

counseling. And finally, changing your thought process to a more positive viewpoint so that you don't continue the pattern in the generation.

Once I became older, my parents went their separate ways until they finally divorced. Our household became a household with just one adult and two children at the time, and that was difficult for Mami. We ended up moving into my grandmother's home, and things became a little more manageable for her financially. Mami had just gotten out of a yearlong drug rehabilitation center and was trying to get back on her feet. I was in the 8th grade and attending Allapattah Middle School, one of the worst schools at the time and located in a tough neighborhood, but nothing I wasn't already accustomed to. Before then, I went to Dunbar Elementary which is located across the street from one of the worst neighborhoods in the city of Miami. Though my neighborhood consisted of both blacks and Hispanics who were dealing with the same social struggles, I had another struggle to deal with. I was light-skinned or "red" as we say in Miami, and I had curly hair. As if life wasn't hard enough already, now I also had to deal with jealousy over something I had no control over—my physical appearance.

Growing up as a fair-skinned Latina with curly, but manageable hair sometimes presented itself as a negative. You see, these were features that many other Latinas did not have, and they were features that some African-American girls typically did not have. As a result, I received mistreatment from black women because of my physical features. And, surprisingly, I also endured hurtful comments and mistreatment from girls of Dominican descent like me. They often said mean things and continuously tried to pick fights with me just because I did not look like them. Yet, as I look at things in hindsight, I feel like these girls prepared me for the rest of my life because I was forced to learn how to deal with jealousy.

Even now, at 35, I am still dealing with jealousy solely because of my physical appearance. Interestingly right now, in the political arena in America, we have a number of women of color in the United States Congress whose physical features, I believe, have evoked discomfort among the majority race simply because their features are not white-like. At any rate, I have learned to counter the jealousy by controlling how I react to other's preconceived notions about me based primarily on my physical appearance. Here is how I do it. Upon meeting people, I do what I can to make them comfortable in my presence. For starters, I use humor to set the atmosphere. I love to laugh, and I love to make others laugh. I engage them quickly in lively conversation so that they will not get the slightest notion that I am stuck up as I was accused of being when I was growing up in the hood. On one level, I believe I automatically try to show how likable I am at the mere greeting of "hello." It's not a bad thing, and it works for me.

Consequently, I usually get the "I didn't know you were this cool and down to earth" kind of comment. On another level, I want to show others that my physical appearance is not the bottom line to who and what I am. I am many things and can get along with mostly anyone. I despise calling it "fitting in" because that comes across like I try to be something I am not just to be embraced by others. Admittedly, in the past, I have tried to 'fit in' only to be met with comments such as "she thinks she's all that." Nothing was further from the truth. So, to keep myself from being offended at the misconceptions of who people thought I was, I would shrug my shoulders like 'oh, well, who cares.' I wanted to ignore them and feel like their comments did not impact me. Truth was I did care. I wanted to prove people wrong. I want to say, "Hey, I am likable, nice, and humble." Through it all, I have learned that the right people—the very ones you should have in your life—will root for you no matter what. They are the ones who will have your back when all seems dark, and you can't find your way.

Most importantly, they are the ones who do not judge you from the outside looking in, but instead take the time to know who you are. Usually those are the people that come into your life and make a difference for the better by feeding the light God put in you and not trying to dim it. For those that are easy to judge, this verse is quite befitting. "Judge not by appearances, but by real judgement" (John 7:24, ESV). Simply put, that means look at the heart. Inner beauty is the true value of a person.

For some of us Latinas, there comes a negative connotation that we are possibly illegals because of our descent. In my case, I have experienced people looking down on me and assuming that I do not understand English due to my physical appearance. There have been plenty of times when I have heard Caucasian women talking about my accent. Some have gone as far as delving into my background by asking me questions about my qualifications to educate children, lead as an administrator, and so on. Oh, they're polite enough with their questions. But I know what the bottom line is for them, which is what gives me the right to teach and discipline their children, live in their neighborhood, make the kind of money I make, and lead other Americans who work under me? Though I was born in the United States, my parents being immigrants gave me firsthand experience of how mean and racist people can be to others that may be different than themselves. Though I can defend myself and articulate my position eloquently with people who question my ability, this is not the case for others. For many immigrants, there comes the scary reality of feeling displaced. They have to adjust to not being around their family, and to new rules and regulations of laws, they may not have been privy to before arriving in the country. They have to get used to the different accents that are so prevalent in the States, not to mention negotiating using the English language. And, they have to prove themselves in the eyes of our society that comes with negative profiling and stereotyping.

My personal experiences of dealing with the triple threat of gender-ism, socioeconomics, and ethnicity have left me with questions about why some Americans lean toward negative perspectives of others whose background is nothing like their own. For example, why is being a woman considered negative? Why is it some view poverty as a negative? And, why is that leading a household as a single parent equally as unfavorable? *(you will have a chance to answer these later)* Sure, we can see that there will be some struggles in some areas, but

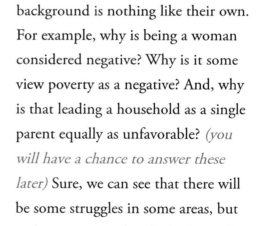

BEING A WOMAN
AND GROWING
IN POVERTY HELPED
ME BECOME A
PERSON OF
CHARACTER AND
INTEGRITY.

even in a two-parent family home, there are struggles. Quite honestly, I do not have the answers to all these questions myself. I do, however, think we should all ask these poignant questions that tend to shroud our judgment of others whose backgrounds vary largely or even slightly from our own. I want to challenge you to look through a positive lens when encountering people from other countries. To me, being a woman and growing in poverty helped me become a person of character and integrity because I know what it means to go without. It made me fight harder to achieve my goals. Yes, it could've been easier, and children should not have to go through some of the things I went through, but in essence, what did not kill me made me stronger.

For the space available, I want you to think of one person or a group of people that is different from you in some way (culture, ethnicity, socioeconomic, etc.). Then I want you to write down all descriptors (e.g., physical appearance, speech, work ethics, foods that may be particular to the group, etc.) that make that person or group of people different from you. Next, record your initial impression and what led you to make those conclusions about this person or group of people. Finally, note any changes in thought about the person or group of people based upon reading this chapter or your own experiences. Strive to be as transparent in your responses as possible. Change can only be made when we are all honest and authentic about our feelings toward one another.

Chapter 5
Questions

Have you ever had to defend who you are due to preconceived judgement? How did you handle that?

My "triple threat" is genderism, low socioeconomic, and ethnicity. Those are issues I still fight daily. What threats do you deal with? How?

Answer the questions at the end of page 84 below.

In retrospect, what have you learned about the effect your upbringing has had on your adult life?

Overall, Chapter Five Reflections

Chapter 6
Results

"The pain that you've been feeling can't compare to the joy that's coming."
- Romans 8:18

Like many others before me, I have finally reached an epiphany about my circumstances that will remain with me for life. Everything I that I ever went through was a test to strengthen me physically, mentally, emotionally, and spiritually. It wasn't necessarily that I had done something wrong or because I was some evil, wicked doer. My trials came to make me a better person, the person God intended me to become.

Now here is another point of encouragement just for you. Dear friend: whatever any of us go through in life isn't supposed to break us; it is supposed to strengthen us to help us birth the purpose we carry within. How many times do we ask ourselves, "Why me?" My conclusion is that life can throw us in so many directions that we begin to move away from God if we don't find our purpose. The reason we go through things is so God can get our attention and ultimately put us back in alignment with what we are supposed to be doing. So, whatever you are facing right now, I believe you will still be standing when it's all over. Be mindful of where you are because there will be a time where you will look back and it will make sense. Many times we don't understand why things happen while we are going through them, but in the end, it will make sense. Yes, even when you feel like you can't advance another step, I believe God will give you that one touch that will make you keep going. It's amazing how God can turn your situation around with just one word. One word from Him, and you can be living your dream.

The question is, will you stay in the fight? Will you embrace the pressure and move forward no matter what? I did. I continued looking for my purpose, for I believed thoroughly in Jeremiah 29:11, where God assures us that He's already planned out our entire life to be prosperous. God wants us to enjoy life abundantly and without measure, but most importantly He wants us to build a friendship with Him. He wants to be our best friend. Absolutely no one is born without purpose and meaning. It is our job to seek our purpose and fulfill it and all we have to do is love Him and talk to Him and listen to Him. If you dedicate your life to Him, He will reveal His secrets to you. The bible says, "Friendship with God is reserved for those who reverence Him. With them alone, he shares the secrets of His promises" (Psalm 25: 14-16).

Like many believers, I always knew God had a special gift with my name on it. I just didn't know how to capture it. I didn't know how to look for it, much less how to recognize it. So many times, we look in the wrong places. We think, if I get this job or if I get this degree or if I get promoted, I will be better off. More often than not we like to say, if I knew someone in there, surely I can get a spot, and that is not true. God doesn't need anyone or anything to put you in the places He desires you to be. He places people in the right position to give way for you to work your purpose. Your job is to figure out what your purpose is, and you can only do that by seeking God and building a friendship with Him.

When I look back at my life and think about the situations that He has brought me through I, know it had to be God! With that in mind, for the past five years, I have been in search of my purpose. I just couldn't shake the feeling that there had to be more in this life for me. I wasn't satisfied, and I had a yearning for something. I was continually feeling God's presence all around me, all the time. I had a family whom I loved with all my heart. I had several degrees, and I had a promising career. Still, something was missing. I wasn't content. So, I did what many of us do when there's a lack of contentment in our lives.

I started to seek Him fervently. I fasted. I prayed. I read the bible. I attended service every Sunday and began to get involved with the church. I started to understand that the yearning...the void, came from a need to be close to our Father who is in heaven. I knew what I needed to do to fulfill that void and I knew it would get me closer to revealing my purpose. In addition, I started listening to inspirational messages and watching sermons on YouTube rather than watching my TV shows or listening to music. I realized that I had to make Him the center of my life, and I couldn't do that just on Sundays. I had to be connected to the source at all times. I felt that I was changing...becoming. It didn't take much for me to get inspired and envision wonderful things happening in my life. I literally cried every day and at night. I wasn't sure what was going on, but I felt the Spirit all the time. I remember now as I write this how the tears flowed so freely. I also remember the time I asked my pastor's wife if she had any idea of why I was always crying lately. I half-way joked with her how I was getting quite annoying with it. Being the kind woman that she is, my dear first lady responded, "Take heart. The Spirit is working. Just let Him flow through you and listen to what He is trying to tell you." Every time I recall her words about what the Spirit was doing in my life, the hairs on my arms rise, and I get a shivering sensation throughout my body. To this day, I am so grateful for her insight and how she has allowed me and guided me to grow. Now, admittedly sometimes the crying was from sadness; but mostly, it was begging to hear God's voice. I began to yearn so much for His attention and literally seek Him. You know how you go to church, and you leave saying, "Wow! I feel like the preacher was talking directly to me." Well, that's exactly how I felt, like 'Yeah, that was for me!' Except I wasn't just saying that after a Sunday service. I was saying it every day about every motivational speech I had watched on YouTube. I said the same about any sign on the street whose wording was even remotely similar to something happening in my life at the moment. I paid close attention to any phrase or conversation between family, friends, and coworkers just in case the Holy Spirit used these conversations to drop information heaven knew that I needed to accomplish the reason for my being. From a spiritual perspective, the "eyes of my understanding" were enlightened like never before. I mean EVERYTHING was 'talking' to me! Even my own thoughts. At times I would just have to stop and say, "thank you, Holy Spirit, for the discernment and confirmation." It was that serious! I began to understand that God was doing a work within me as a way of preparing me for my 'next,' whatever that was to be. Sometimes God prepares me from the inside out. This is quite the opposite of how mankind would do things. For example, in preparation of some event we will attend, we prepare ourselves on the outside. We find the most beautiful attire to wear, a makeup artist to get our makeup just right, and the best hairstylist to give us a 'do' the world will never forget. Yet, all that outside preparation is useless against a special task God made us for.

Additionally, outside preparation is no match for the pressure points that will definitely come. Cosmetic fixes are not known for helping anyone embrace pressure, as my book cover encourages. With all that God is doing inside of me, I know that I am becoming everything He meant for me to be, and I am walking in my purpose, and so should you.

GOD PLANTS, WE GROW

In the summer of 2018, I registered to attend a women's conference sponsored by my church. It was a two-night event featuring speakers who were gems. These were real women of God teaching and motivating other women. Many of us shed tears like never before on those days, and many were released from bondage of one kind or another. In so many words, we gave eviction notices to depression, low self-esteem, doubt, fear, abuse, mental illnesses, and all things that are not of God. That experience, the women there, the speakers who saw more in me than I did in myself, pushed me to write this book! I am forever grateful! Let this be a lesson to all that we should always be around people that will pour into us and see things in us that we may not see in ourselves.

An important, life-saving message that I learned during that conference is that our Heavenly Father God has planted a seed (purpose) within us. From a natural standpoint, every seed needs a host of some sort in which to grow. It also needs to be watered and exposed to light. Our spiritual growth stages are similar to those of a natural seed. We need people in our lives that will water us and shed light on us in order for us to grow that seed and bear fruit.

When God created each of us, He was meticulous in the type of seed He planted. He made sure that we would be able to bear the fruit that will grow out of it. That's why it is essential to tend to the flock we have. We have to ensure the people around us are there to water and to shed light on that seed. That is the only way we will grow. We weren't meant to be in this world alone; therefore, we need people in our corner that will nourish our spirit, encourage our passion, and help us bloom. If we are not careful, we could get stunted and delayed. The good Word says that where two or more gather in agreement, God is in the midst, and what they ask for, it will be done. So, I ask you. Who is watering you? Who is pouring into you? Who is shining the light on you? We cannot grow alone. There is no such thing as anyone reaching purpose without the other.

> DEAR FRIENDS, WE NEED EACH OTHER TO FULFILL GOD'S PURPOSE IN OUR LIVES.

So, if you are a loner trying to achieve much, you will not reach the heights you were born to reach without help. Life will not work for you that way. Dear friends, we need each other to fulfill God's purpose in our lives. With that said, who's in your circle? Who will touch and agree with you?

PERFECT RESULTS FROM IMPERFECT PEOPLE

After going through the hurricanes, tornadoes, and earthquakes life has thrown at me, I stayed the course. I continued to explore God and His word and applied it directly to my everyday life. What I found was that LOVE was the answer. Yes, it's that simple, love.

My father betrayed my mother and abandoned me. Years later, I had to find the courage to put aside all of my hurt and pain in order to care for him as if he were my child. I didn't realize it then, but there was a lesson in all that… forgiveness! I had to forgive him in order to move forward in my life. This did not come easy. There were mental, emotional, and physical struggles. I wanted to give up every time I got frustrated. Every time I couldn't see the point in doing so much for someone who didn't appreciate my time or my giving. Every day, I was faced with the same challenge. That is, I had to choose to forgive him, because forgiveness is not automatic. It is a daily choice on our part. It is a conscious decision to forgive. In order to do this effectively, I had to take matters into my own hands. I decided to dig deeper into Papi's life in hopes of understanding of his upbringing and his family traditions. I hoped that doing this would enlighten me on some of his ways and why he raised me the way he did.

I had to look at his past to understand why he was the way he was. For starters, I asked a few questions about him to help me pinpoint what made him tick. I knew he could tick others off with no problem! But I wanted to know what made him tick. I started with these questions: What kind of formal education did my father have? What kind of formal education did his father have? What type of environment and upbringing were each of them exposed to?

Digging into his history helped me become more compassionate toward him and realize that sometimes people just do the best they can with what they know. Papi had a sixth-grade education, while his father had no formal education to speak of. Papi grew up in a hut in Santo Domingo, Dominican Republic, where the two rooms it had were separated with blankets, not doors. Papi and his siblings wore shoes only when on special outings. Otherwise, they walked on dirt roads without shoes. Papi said he didn't even wear his shoes when he did go to a neighborhood celebration for fear of wasting away the soles of his shoes. Instead, he saw where something as simple as a pair of shoes could bring him value. He wore them to go fishing. He would go fishing and bring some home to cook for the family and good fishing trips where he'd catch a many. He would sell his catch to make a profit for much-needed income.

My grandfather also had a few women in his life at one time and many children. It is not uncommon there to have many wives and many children. Papi is one of at least thirteen children that I know of. From what I could gather, many, many nights, my grandfather's clan of children went to bed hungry. They were very poor, and all of them had to manage how to bring in something to help maintain the household.

I never had the privilege of getting to know his mother. She died while giving birth to him due to complications that were beyond the healing hands of any doctor. I can only imagine if he feels any guilt about that. I am sure that it must have had a negative effect on him growing up and even as an adult.

In unveiling some unpleasant events in Papi's life, I realized a few things. One of them is this: he did the best he could do with what he had. I had to look back at the information I uncovered and ask myself what real knowledge did he have on how to be a good father? A good husband? He had neither of these as examples growing up. Therefore, once he married and had children of his, who could he mimic as a doting father and loving husband? No one. I have had to accept that. Quite honestly, I admit that I have had to wonder exactly how deep the pain was for him to go without the neces-

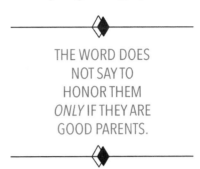

THE WORD DOES NOT SAY TO HONOR THEM *ONLY* IF THEY ARE GOOD PARENTS.

sities of life and the struggle that inevitably comes from not having the love and caretaking of both parents. The necessities such as grade school education, three meals a day, shoes, and a proper home in which water could not seep through the roof was totally missing in his childhood. It is no wonder that with such humble beginnings, he would undoubtedly fall short of parenting his own children appropriately one day.

I became compassionate and sympathetic to Papi. Tears filled my eyes as I think of all the struggles he must've faced. Yet, sometimes I look at my own life. When I don't know how to do something, I find the answer. I research, I dig, I ask. I know to prepare for potential barriers, and I think twice about my actions to ensure that if anything goes wrong, I can handle it. Even with my own life struggles, I still have the mental capacity to think ahead and make wise decisions. As I continued to think about this, I decided to read about how the environment one lives in can shape one's brain process. It all started to come together for me. I realized once again that Papi did the best he could with what he had.

In time, I made peace with Papi's shortcomings as a dad by embracing his story and his struggles. This man may not have answers for me, but he will have to answer one day to God. Until then, my duty was to honor him regardless of whether I felt he was a good father or not because that's what the Word of God tells me to do and that will be my answer on judgment day. Out of my love for God, my Savior, I am determined to obey and to follow His commandments. God says we must honor our mother and father; in turn, years of life will be added unto onto us. The Word does not say to honor them only if they are good parents. No, we are to honor them in spite of. Therefore, I learned to forgive him and to understand his life journey so that, in turn, I can be a better parent to my daughter and break the cycle. Forgiving Him has been one of the most important struggles I've had to embrace. I also realized that forgiveness is a journey, I didn't just wake up, and the feeling of despair and abandonment suddenly disappeared. No. Every day, it is a conscious decision to acknowledge my feelings, meet them with sincerity, allow myself to feel them, and then make a mental decision to move forward in love. That's one of the greatest lessons I've learned on my own journey toward my finding my purpose.

Papi taught me the importance of forgiveness, and from Mami, I have learned quite a few other lessons. Living with, I learned many things. As I navigate Mami's life, one obvious lesson is quite simple. Stay away from drugs! This much I picked up from going on drug runs with her. I also learned to be aware of my surroundings and to look for the signs of danger and/or people that may not be safe to hang around. I learned to study my Mami and her behaviors at certain moments. I knew when she wanted to get a hit because her eyes would just glisten, and she'd look around anxiously. She would begin to pace and just seemed to move around too much in the very limited space of our little apartment. I also knew when she was going in the bathroom to use the toilet or when it was to get a quick hit. When she would come out the bathroom, I can tell she was high because she would be very calm and nostalgic. I could also smell the scent of the drug swarming around in the bathroom and seeping out through the cracks of the door. I can smell it now as I'm writing this. I don't think I can ever forget that smell.

Regardless of whatever she was not, my mother was and still is an awesome woman. In retrospect, I admire how hard she worked to keep up with her responsibilities even as a drug addict. I would say she never missed a beat. Now, as a survivor and rehabilitated drug addict, she continues to be a woman of God, for which I am so grateful for. Her faith in times vulnerability, struggles, and victories have kept us her and those around her in line with God's word. Even in her dark moments when it seemed drug abuse would take over her life and drown out memories of her best days, God was with her. Many horrible things could've happened to her while she was high on crack, but God kept her and gave her the will to choose Him and her children over drugs. I am forever grateful.

As I did with Papi, I had to come to peace with some things Mami did that was quite unsettling for a child to deal with. One of the most difficult times of my life was having to live with Papi while Mami was checking into a live-in drug rehabilitation center. I felt that she had left me. I felt abandoned, even though I knew this was the best choice for her to get clean and straighten up her life. I was proud of her for going, but I also felt selfish. I wanted to be with Mami more than anything. More importantly, I wanted to care for her and watch over her. I wanted to keep her safe as I did when I went on drug runs with her. I just wanted to be with her at all times. But I knew I had to suck it up. I had to live with Papi and my stepmother, who I wasn't a fan of simply because she didn't respect Mami. I fully understand now and accept that her leaving me behind and going to a live-in rehabilitation center was a huge decision and sacrifice she had to make. How else was she going to conquer something that had stolen way too much of her time and health? To this day, I have never asked her. I imagine, now as a parent myself, that there was indeed a deep sorrow that she felt from having to be away from me, her daughter, for any given period of time. The strength she had to have to endure withdrawal from missing me and drugs I'm sure came with no small consequence, I'm sure.

I remember watching real-life documentaries on drug addiction, such as Intervention. The withdrawal process drug addicts in the show had to endure was gut-wrenching! Yet, necessary. It's all part of the road to healing. I can imagine the feeling of loneliness that crept into her room on some nights. I think about it, and I can't help but smirk because, if you knew my mother, you wouldn't ever think she had ever felt lonely or ashamed. That woman is a firecracker! So full of life!

To this day, I still watch episodes of Intervention whenever I can. My husband always wonders why I like watching that show. No matter how many times I tell him that I like to watch it because it gives me insight into what Mami and other family members went through, he still doesn't understand. I always cry watching those episodes. They bring back so many memories and so many feelings from my past. I remember being anxious that Mami will walk out the door for drugs and not ever come back afraid that something would happen to her. In the end, when they give the update, I'm always rooting for the addict. It gives me great joy when the addict featured gain sobriety and can return to their families' whole again.

HEALING COMES FOR ME, TOO

Being violated and subsequently feeling ashamed of myself over something that was not my fault is something I struggled with for a long time. In hindsight, I know that part of the reason I looked to men for reassurance and permission to do certain things was that I just didn't feel like I was good enough. In a way, I felt like I was dirty and had to make up for it by being obedient and seeking refuge in a man's arms. Being sexually abused gave me one more reason to feel unwanted in this unsacred, unforgiving world. Through this experience, though it took me longer than I would've liked, I learned to love myself. I learned that I deserved to have life's best. I learned that repetition is not always a positive thing. For instance, I was attracting the same kind of men due to my 'energy,' which was a negative 'energy.' I knew the cycle had to be broken. But how?

 During my senior year in college, I did a lot of necessary soul-searching. I read books, I went to church, and I developed a relationship with MYSELF! I learned to love me for my past. You read that right, my past. I confronted that little girl inside of me who was ignored by her grandmother when she told her she had been molested and grew her up! I finally let her have her "moment" to feel what she had a right to feel, and then I set her free! I was no longer bound by that little girl whom I felt so badly for. I was able to look her in the face and told her that she was beautiful, worthy and that she could let go now.

God seems to give these tasks to His strongest warriors, those whom He has called to greatness. My dad abandoned me, yet I came back to help him at his time of need. Interestingly, I had to help this uncle of mine as well. This man was incarcerated at the local county jail but was immediately detained by ICE (Immigration and Customs Enforcement) due to having a criminal record and an expired residence card. Living in America over 40 years, you'd think he would've become a Unites States citizen, but he didn't. So here he was labeled an illegal and facing deportation. He had been detained for some time and the family gathered money to get him legal representation that specializes in immigration law.

The lawyer happily took the money, but not much was done. No one could spare any more money and therefore he decided to represent himself. We all knew that was a bad idea. He's never been the sharpest knife in the drawer by far! My aunt (coincidentally, the same one he molested in the past) said she would speak on his behalf in court. As the proceedings began, my aunt, who is usually very outspoken turned out to be the least supportive that day. Her language was not strong nor convincing when speaking to the judge. I was itching to stand up and speak for him instead. I don't know if it was just my nature for helping others and being a great debater, or if I wanted to help just because I know my Mami and the others wanted him to stay in the United States. In the end, our family decided that I should speak on his behalf at the next court hearing, and so I did. I spoke well. I showed the court that he was employed and other necessary depositions in his defense.

Additionally, the prosecutors failed to prove their case against him for crimes he supposedly committed 20 years before. When all was said and done, he won and was released from jail the following day! In essence, I had won his case. I will never forget the judge looking at me in my face and asking me why I had not pursued a career in law. He was amused by my wittiness and how I made the prosecutor look like an amateur. So there I was, the victim defending her molester. I knew for sure at that point; I had been healed. Because I had no hate in my heart for that man, that act was what forgiveness looks like. But I also knew I had more work to do, more healing within needed to take place as soon as possible. Two times I have saved people that let me down in a significant way. Papi, who abandoned me, and I eventually had to care for and my uncle, who defiled me, and then I had to save from deportation. Why was I so willing to help these men who hurt me so badly? I had to figure that out on my own.

Being the oldest, I learned to be a protective, attentive, and responsible person. My siblings were entirely dependent on me for a considerable number of years, but as I got older and wanted to hang out with friends, I started to hate being the oldest. I had to do everything. I did my job so well that my mom bought me a car on my 15th birthday! I was happy, but the responsibilities toward caring for my siblings and taking care of the house did not end. With having a car came more responsibilities. I went grocery shopping. I cooked, I did my sister's hair. I picked up both my brother and my sister from after school care every day, cleaned the house, and helped with homework. It was indeed a fulltime job. I am 35 years old now, and sometimes, I still don't like being the oldest even among now adult siblings. When my Mami calls me, I sometimes look at the phone like "Hmmm…I wonder what happened now." Most times, it's usually just ordinary conversations. Other times, it's "You need to talk to your brother...or your sister did this or that...call her!" I don't want to talk to them about whatever they got going on a lot of times, because I know they both need to go through their growing pains. Just like me, I didn't always listen to advice, and sometimes I had to see it for myself. Still, I try to guide them as best I can and as much as I can without getting all in their personal business.

Being the big sister and having so many responsibilities fall on me gave me a look into motherhood and life in general at a young age. Thanks to early 'motherhood' with my young siblings and trying to help my Mami around the house, I learned to manage my time to fit in chores, hobbies, studying, and completing homework, among other things. Viewing life through the lens of responsibility at an early age exposed me to great wisdom and set me up for success for the various phases of life I had yet to experience. Many would look at this taking on early adulthood as a negative. At times I even saw it that way. It had a positive side also. It allowed me to see both of my siblings at different phases of their lives and affording me the pleasure of sharing special, distinct moments with each of them.

Upon high school graduation, I left the nest to venture out to college and be the guinea pig being the first one to leave home for post-secondary education in hopes of graduating with a bachelor's degree and become a strong, educated professional. I made many errors in choosing courses, with financial aid and just college life in general. However, I always felt that my tribulations during my college years were not in vain. The amount of student loans I racked up, the amount of unneeded credit hours by changing majors too many times, and even the knowledge of out-of-state tuition versus in-state tuition allowed me to guide my siblings should they want to pursue post-secondary education. I hoped they would follow in my footsteps as I was setting a precedent for what it meant to reach for your dreams and 'hang in there' no matter what. I realized after I graduated that my purpose was bigger than me. I even became a school of education advisor at Miami-Dade College at one point and I loved advising students on what courses to take, in what sequence, and why. The point is this: nothing we go through, good or bad, happens in vain. In this way, we pay it forward. I think the great poet Maya Angelou said it best, "When you learn, teach. When you get, give."

TRUST, THEN BELIEVE

When people show you who they are, believe them the first time (another Angelou jewel). Through my battle surviving domestic violence, I learned to trust actions. I learned to trust my instincts, my gut. I learned to trust the different faces and nuisances people make. I learned to trust certain utterances, and uh-oh's people make under their breath. And, yes, I learned to look for and trust peoples' initial words and actions right at the moment of introduction.

Life is not a baseball game, but a word or deed spoken or done against you can hit as hard as a blow to the head from a speeding, inerrant baseball. That blow to your head or your body could've taken your life or caused some sort of devastation were it not for the grace of GOD! For those who believe they have been struck out by domestic violence or any other violence to their bodies, I want to encourage you get out of that situation immediately! No one has a right to lay a hand on you the first time, much less a third time! As in baseball, consider that particular 'laying on of hands' a strike and an OUT at the same time! Remember, God did not create you to get beaten on. Domestic violence is a serious matter and it is not to be taken lightly. Many people, women in particular, have suffered and/or died at the hands of their mate or partner. Understand that your life has a purpose and a calling. Not everyone will understand what a precious diamond you are. Typically, what people do not understand, they become fearful of or jealous of.

In some cases, they may even plot your demise instead of appreciating your beauty and worth. They may even start to question themselves, and when they don't feel like they are worthy or can keep up with you, they tend to take their insecurities out on you. They want to bring you down to their level. In short, dear friends, learn to detect the signs of abuse and get out!

The thing about domestic violence is that many times the perpetrator is not someone others see as violent. How many times have you viewed on the news neighbors and friends refer to a domestic violence offender as "nice"? It usually goes something like this, "I used to see him with the children all the time and walking the dog. He was always so respectful and nice. I would've never thought he could do something like this." Out of their own need to fool others, they put on a facade in public. They wear that facade to the point where even the victim starts to believe that fakery. They are such excellent actors that suddenly the victim begins to think the violence against her may have been her fault. Once the victim takes on the guilt of being victimized, it becomes increasingly difficult to leave the abuser. It is equivalent to trying to break free of the devil's power and dominance. For me, this is precisely why having a relationship with the Most High God is essential. When I came to understand the Word of God, I began to see how God does not allow the devil to take control of your life. My study of the Word also helped me see that in our times of despair, God sends His angels to protect and give

WHETHER YOU WERE THROWN INTO A PIT OR YOU CLIMBED INTO THAT PIT YOURSELF, YOU HAVE THE POWER TO GET OUT AND MOVE IN THE WILL OF GOD.

us comfort. Before you read the next chapter, I want you to understand this one life-changing fact. Jehovah God is the only God there is. He did not bring you this far in your life journey to forsake you. God has given every one of His children the spirit of power, love, and boldness (2 Timothy 1:7). Let that truth sink in, then rise up and get out of toxic situations, circumstances, environments, relationships, spirits, and anything that is not conducive to your purpose.

The bottom line is this: whether you were thrown into a pit as Joseph or whether you climbed into that pit yourself, you still have the power to get out and move in the will of God.

Chapter 6
Questions

In what ways have your circumstances made you better? Stronger?

When you feel like there has got to be more to life or feel lost, what do you do to uplift yourself?

We can't give what we don't have. Who do you have in your life that pours into your spirit? Is it feeding you rather than starving you? If you don't have anyone positive fighting on your behalf, how will you find that person?

In life, we must forgive to release hurt and pain. Whom have you forgiven? How has it helped you along your journey?

Overall, Chapter Six Reflections

Chapter 7
Under Pressure

Each of the following processes involves unprecedented, unbearable pressure. Ironically, the resulting product each process produces would not bear the worth and flawlessness it does, were it not for the intense pressure. In simple lay person's terms, no pressure, no worth.

Read the following three processes. Then ask yourself, 'which one would I be able to withstand'?

THE MAKING OF A DIAMOND

To form a diamond, tremendous temperatures and pressures are required. How high is the temperature, you wonder? Try 2000 degrees Fahrenheit. And what about the pressure involved? Well, scientists believe that diamonds were formed about 90 miles below the earth's surface.

Interestingly, they made their way above ground via volcanic eruptions. Can you imagine the pressure it takes for a volcano to erupt, much less to the point where it brings to the surface the world's hardest natural

d

material? And, did I mention that it takes billions of years for natural diamonds to form. Now, that's a lot of pressure and time to bring something to perfection!

Have you ever wondered why God made the diamond so hard? I have. Think about it for a while. He deliberately made the diamond-hard enough and enduring enough to cut through other wear-bearing materials with no resistance to it at all. When comparing the rough patches of intense pressure that I went through a few times, I have concluded that our heavenly Father has tried to show us a few things with the making of the diamond. For one, He has made us to endure many things until His perfect timing brought an end to them. As for each of you, I believe He has given you the grace to withstand circumstances and come out of them hardened. Not to a point where we are cruel to other people, but so that we realize that we are more than conquerors and not just anything will be able to keep His people down for too long. And in the case of forming the diamond into perfection, God took His sweet time. He does the same where we are concerned. Our Father is aware of our circumstances, a number of which have brought on the burning heat in our lives. However, He will pull us out of the 'fire' at just the right moment and will have no choice but to glorify his name.

THE SCIENCE OF CORN POPPING

Popcorn kernels contain oil and water with starch, surrounded by a hard and durable outer coating. When popcorn is heated, the water inside the kernel tries to expand into steam, but it cannot escape through the coating (i.e., the hull part) of the seed. The hot oil and steam gelatinize the starch inside the popcorn kernel, making it softer and more pliable. When the popcorn reaches a temperature of 180 C (356 F), the pressure inside the kernel is sufficient enough to rupture the popcorn hull, essentially turning the kernel inside-out. The pressure inside the kernel is released very quickly, expanding the proteins and starch inside the popcorn kernel into a foam, which sets into the tasty, familiar popcorn puff. Retrieved from the web https://www.thoughtco.com/how-does-popcorn-pop-607429, August 31, 2019, 12:47PM.

PRESSURE COOKER

Pressure cookers are a convenient kitchen appliance used to cook food quickly with the power of steam pressure. Even without pressure, steam conducts heat and cooks faster than dry air. However, with increased pressure, the steam can rise above its usual maximum temperature and cook even faster. These factors make steam pressure cooking faster than baking, steaming, or boiling.

So, which process would you like to undergo? If you're anything like me, you'd answer 'not one of them'! Yet pressure in life is inevitable. Consider Jesus' teaching on His being the vine, and the Father is the husbandman (the One who cultivates; the One who is the Master of the house; worker of the soil) of the vineyard. We, His children, are the vineyard or soil that He masters. As the husbandman, our Father decides what kind of pressure to add to the purpose of our being. That means He may turn up the heat if you will, but never ever to burn you or consume you in order to transform you into the person He needs you to be to carry out your purpose. If it seems the heat in your life has been turned up, it's because that amount of 'pressure' is needed to mold and shape you into a copy of His Son, our Lord, and Savior. Sometimes that pressure will be quick, as is the case for pressure cookers cooking their contents into the deliciousness that will be just right for the waiting consumer. At other times, it may seem you have been immersed in a particular circumstance for ages, as is the case for the diamond in a rough. God waits at just the right moment to release it to a place above ground where it can be found used for its purpose. See, even His precious materials have a purpose. For the Lord, nothing exists on its own. Everything and everyone was made for His divine purpose. Therefore, pressure is added to build muscle, stamina, foundation, endurance.

Here's another biblical illustration that discusses our being prepared

> PRESSURE POINTS ARE NEEDED TO SHAPE US AND ENABLE US TO DO WHAT THE FATHER HAS CALLED US TO DO.

for service to Him. Jeremiah 18, Isaiah 29, and Isaiah 64 each speak of the potter (i.e., the Lord) and the clay (the people of God). Before being shaped, clay must be prepared. Kneading helps to ensure an even moisture content throughout the body of the clay. Once a clay body has been kneaded and de-aired or wedged, it is shaped by a variety of techniques. After it has been formed, it is dried, and then the potter fires it in a kiln, subjecting it to the highest amount of heat or pressure it needs to maintain the shape.

At no time during the shaping or baking in the kiln does the clay say to the potter turn the pressure off. Instead, the clay takes the pressure it needs to fulfill the purpose for which the potter made it. Such is life for us. Pressure points are necessary to shape us and enable us to do what the Father has called us to do. Otherwise, we would fall apart at the least amount of pressure that He applies to our journey when we are in the middle of fulfilling our purpose. Thanks to Him, the pressure he adds to our lives not only helps us push through the hard times, it enables us to thrive past the pressure and into becoming who He created us to be.

Epilogue
When is enough, enough?

W hat is your point of pressure? At what point do you say to your-self, there's got to be more to life than this." Some of you may define your pressure point as that certain feeling you get when you are doing all you can for everyone else, while you feel like you are a mouse running on the fastest Ferris wheel, but going nowhere. To make matters worse, everybody around you seems to be experiencing progress, which has only left you behind.

Have you ever wondered why you're always so tired? Why are you still struggling? Why are you still pinching pennies? Why are people always dependent on you? Why? Why? Why? The answer is simple. God has anointed you. Everyone cannot handle pressure well. Things that you've been through could have sent someone else into a deep depression, provoking them to use illegal drugs to cope with the day ahead. Worse yet, the pressure may have led them to suicide. But you, darling, are a gem. You are that diamond in the rough that withstood the intensity of the heat! And, now spiritually, emotionally, and physically, you are so much better than before the pressure point came.

d

You were born to uplift, to create, and to empower others. That's why everyone is looking at you! It's hard to understand this sometimes because we feel like we keep getting dealt a lousy hand. We think that we keep getting looked over after all the work we've put in. As a result, we tend to minimize the blessings along the way because we give more power to the situation rather than to the process toward victory!

As for me, I indeed endured some very dark times. Like some of you reading this book, I've felt lonely, betrayed, used, and abused. But happily, I am still here. From breaking through my own hard times, my advice to you is not to dwell on the inconveniences so much. Instead, acknowledge the situation, the struggle, learn the lessons that come from the circumstance, make peace with it, bury it, and move on! Walk into your new destiny with the mindset of a victorious warrior. You are a diamond, once buried in mud, and now shining ever so bright. I believe that's how life is turning out for me. Just think: I had an uncle to molest me. Yet, I wound up being the one family member to save him from deportation. Being away from my family to go to college— the ones that I cooked for, picked up from school, etc.—was tough. Many times I thought about quitting college and come back home, but I didn't. And, too, being different, that is a city girl from Miami who wasn't either black or white, but an Afro Latina attending an HBCU was a hard pill to swallow for others.

Nevertheless, I stayed the course and graduated. Then there were all these doubts about being the caretaker of my aging, uncaring father. Even in that case, I bit the bullet and cared for him better than any nurse with training. All in all, to have succumbed to the madness would've been my own demise. I deliberately chose to fly. I decided to embrace the pressure and soar. And, in every circumstance, I decided the way of the Lord, the trusted the Potter of my life.

Right now, I will not pretend to know the why of every circumstance. Perhaps someday, God will show me why it had to be me, why I had to be the chain breaker, the one to break generational curses of poverty and drug addiction. I started Revolutionary Diamond Book Publishing Company to change the status quo of how things normally turn out for my family. I wanted my daughter to see that her mother is a woman who, despite the rocks that have been thrown at her, decided to continue the good fight of faith and soar. I wanted her to see her mom take every rock thrown at her and build a monument. I wanted her to understand that those rocks were the building blocks that allowed me to climb to greatness. I used them to make a concrete ladder for my latter! I still use those rocks today to continue treading and defying the odds that I, the daughter of a 9th-grade dropout and of a man who only has the education of a 6th grader, of pure immigrants in the United States can still be an achiever! Can graduate with multiple college degrees. Can become a certified life coach. A certified teacher. An educational leader. A writing coach. Even an author.

EPILOGUE ACTIVITY

This last activity is more of a dare than anything else. By writing this book about some things I struggled to overcome, I took a huge leap of faith in telling bits and pieces of my story. Now, I dare you to do the same. Remember, your journey is somebody else's lesson. Your journey is not meant for you to keep to yourself. Do you have the courage? Will you answer the call? Someone is waiting to hear your story to be released from bondage. I can coach you, so let's go! Go ahead—write that book!

Overall Reflections

PRESSUREPOINT
ADVERSITIES STRENGTHEN AND PUSH YOU TO YOUR DESTINY

Giving Things That Matter

Visit our online home at revolutionary-diamond.com to get your free gift: a printable Study Guide to go along with Pressure Point. This guide is equipped with the questions written throughout the book. It gives you more room to write and reflect about your personal journey. Here's the CHALLENGE:

I want you to "pay it forward". If my personal journey has been a blessing to you... if you have learned anything...if you have been inspired...if you have shed a tear or have gotten emotional...consider giving your copy to someone you think could benefit from the lessons you found in Pressure Point.

Using this printable guide allows you the freedom to write your own truths and the ability to pass along your copy of "Pressure Point" to someone who needs to hear how all of their trials and tribulations are a part of God's plan. Give it to someone who needs to learn about how they can turn their defeats into victory as they are a part of God's plan. THEIR GOD-GIVEN PURPOSE.

Download your free guide from revolutionary-diamond.com now.